DAY TRADING

FROM UNDERSTANDING **RISK MANAGEMENT** AND
CREATING **TRADE PLANS** TO RECOGNIZING **MARKET**
PATTERNS AND USING **AUTOMATED SOFTWARE**,
AN ESSENTIAL PRIMER IN **MODERN DAY TRADING**

101

DAVID BORMAN

Adams Media

New York London Toronto Sydney New Delhi

Aadamsmedia

Adams Media
An Imprint of Simon & Schuster, Inc.
57 Littlefield Street
Avon, Massachusetts 02322

First Adams Media hardcover edition JANUARY 2018

ADAMS MEDIA and colophon are trademarks of Simon and Schuster.

For information about special discounts for bulk purchases, please contact Simon & Schuster Special Sales at 1-866-506-1949 or business@simonandschuster.com.

The Simon & Schuster Speakers Bureau can bring authors to your live event. For more information or to book an event contact the Simon & Schuster Speakers Bureau at 1-866-248-3049 or visit our website at www.simonspeakers.com.

Interior design by Katrina Machado

Manufactured in the United States of America

6 2021

Library of Congress Cataloging-in-Publication Data has been applied for.

ISBN 978-1-5072-0581-5
ISBN 978-1-5072-0582-2 (ebook)

DEDICATION

This book is dedicated to my mom, Cynthia, and my two brothers, Bill and Ted, all of whom have been there for me during the writing of this and all my other books. They've been there through all my non-stop talk about this or that economic theory, they've been there for countless late-night writing sessions, they've been there through the good times and the bad... In short, they've always been there for me.

ACKNOWLEDGMENTS

In the writing of this book there was much help: I'd like to thank my editors at Simon & Schuster, Eileen Mullan and Peter Archer, and the huge work they did to get this book to press. I'd also like to thank the editorial board, because they liked the proposal and gave me enough time to write it. I'd like to thank all my current and previous bosses, who gave me the chance to work at their companies, the chance to learn, and the chance to grow in my career in finance and the markets. Last, I'd like to thank my bestie best, Ilona, for encouraging me to keep writing until I made every deadline.

CONTENTS

INTRODUCTION

Just what is day trading?

When people hear the word *trading*, they usually think of the stock market and of the kind of thing that happens with their 401(k) accounts (or other retirement accounts). But that's not really stock trading; it's *investing*. People who trade stocks don't buy into a 401(k) or brokerage account with a preset amount with each payroll check. Instead, they buy and sell stocks in order to make a profit.

Many traders think long term and buy and hold stocks for some time—in fact, sometimes for years. But there's another kind of trading, and that's what we're going to talk about in the following pages: *day trading.*

In one sense, day trading is exactly what it sounds like. Day traders buy and sell stock within a twenty-four-hour period. Sometimes they hold the stock for only minutes, sometimes for a few hours. But in the end, day trading is the process of starting a trading session at the beginning of the day in 100 percent cash, buying and selling securities during the day for profits, and making sure to sell off all the account holdings by the end of the day, thereby returning to all cash at the end of the trading session.

Day traders buy and sell stocks many times in a single day. Their goal is to capture gains and book profits on their trades during the hours the markets are open. Day after day, month after month, they repeat the process of starting in cash, trading, booking profits, and ending the day in cash. Although the profit on each trade is often relatively small, the *volume* of their trades allows day traders to book huge profits on average-sized accounts over the year. As the profits come in, the trader's account grows in value, allowing larger trades.

Another distinguishing feature of day trading is the use of "leverage" to amplify purchasing power. When day traders use leverage (also called margin accounts) in their trading accounts, they are essentially buying stock or securities with credit. This is much like purchasing a house with only a 10 or 20 percent down payment and a mortgage for the balance. In the case of day trading, the trader puts up cash or other securities for the down payment, and the brokerage account lends him money to buy more stock or other securities. This means that with the right management, relatively small accounts can book sizeable profits.

Finally, one of the best qualities of day trading is the availability of twenty-four-hour markets. Day trading can be done whenever the markets are open: for stocks, this usually means 7:30 a.m. to 2 p.m. Eastern US time. But while the US stock market is only open during the day, other markets are open twenty-four hours a day, six days a week. This means you can keep your regular day job while building up your skills at trading in your off hours. You can trade on your own time, whether late in the evening before bed or early in the morning before work. You can even trade on a smartphone or a tablet; brokerage houses offer sophisticated trading platforms for both. Trading can be done anywhere you have access to the

Internet: at the coffee shop, at your home office. It doesn't have to take a lot of time either. You might spend only an hour a day looking for trades and only trade two to four times a week, searching for only the best trades that offer the best profits. It's really up to you how you want to build your trading business.

This book will walk you through the basic concepts of how to start day trading, from opening and funding your trading account, looking for profitable trades, knowing when to exit a trade for a good amount of profit, and steering clear of bad trades. You will learn the differences between day trading, short-term trading, and investing, and you will see what you'll need to get up and running in your day trading account to make your trading manageable, enjoyable, and profitable. All it takes is a bit of knowledge and insight, and with a little time and practice, you'll be able to read the signals of the market, you'll know how to determine the good trades from the bad trades, and you'll start booking profits.

Chapter 1

Introduction to Markets and Trading

Trading, day trading, and investing are terms that are used to describe the buying and selling of financial products that are traded electronically. Whether they be stocks, commodities such as oil or gold, or foreign currency, day traders and traders use computers to buy and sell in what is called the financial markets. Most people are familiar with the US markets such as the stock market, but the financial markets are worldwide, and it is possible to trade stocks from a European company, gold warehoused in Asia, or the currencies of developing nations. What ties them all together is that the trading is done electronically and can be done from your home computer or, in many cases, from your tablet or smartphone.

FUNCTIONS OF THE MARKETS

Market Makers and Market Pricing

The markets are the grouping of financial trading people, products, and platforms. By this I mean the market is the loose association of professional and personal traders and investors who carry out both short-term and long-term trades and investments in financial products such as stocks, foreign moneys, and commodities such as gold and oil. These are the market participants, buying and selling electronically or face to face, within the confines of the accepted rules and regulations of trading and investing. Keep in mind that the market refers to the industry as a whole, not just stocks, bonds, or other traded instruments.

Say the word *markets*, and most people think of the tumultuous "pits" that we often see on television and in pictures of the New York Stock Exchange (NYSE). Dozens of traders are closely gathered, waving their hands wildly while yelling out buy and sell orders. These "pits" are on the floor of the stock exchanges. At these locations, the traders are sometimes market makers.

MARKET MAKERS

Market markers are traders whose profit is made from buying and selling all available stock in which they are dealers. They are the first to buy and sell all orders coming through the exchange floor for that stock, and they earn a commission on each trade. The downside of this is that if the market has a bad day, they still have to buy all shares of their specialty stock, whatever the price. This is true even if their order book is full and they have very few buyers. Market makers facilitate the efficient and orderly operation of the investment markets in good times and bad.

Many market makers work for large firms such as Morgan Stanley or Merrill Lynch; others are employed by private account holders who own a "seat" on the exchange. Having a seat allows them to put a person on the floor of the exchange to get in on the trading action.

On the floors of the exchanges, trades are often made in bulk orders of one thousand shares or more, but floor traders can handle smaller trades (hundred-share lots or even smaller). Floor traders trade for their own account or for firms that buy shares for their client's accounts. In either case, the motivation of market makers is the access to all trades that come through the floor and a commission on each trade that they handle for clients. Market makers are strictly regulated by the Securities and Exchange Commission (SEC), the Financial Industry Regulatory Authority (FINRA), and the National Futures Association (NFA). The SEC is the government body that polices, investigates, and prosecutes financial and market fraud in the United States. FINRA and NFA are self-governing industry watchdogs that monitor and regulate all US-based stock, foreign exchange market, and futures professionals.

Fiduciary Care

While market makers are a form of broker, only FINRA/NFA brokers registered to provide "care of custodial control of client accounts" are required to provide a fiduciary service: meaning only these registered brokers are required to put their client's financial needs above their own.

Determining Price

In addition to providing a physical or electronic gathering place for buyers and sellers of financial products such as stocks, foreign currency, and futures, the world's marketplaces help buyers and sellers determine the current price of what's being traded. Trading screens scattered throughout the trading floor of the exchanges show a buy and a sell price for each stock. The prices are updated constantly so that traders can see what a trade is worth moment to moment, allowing them what is called *price discovery*. The buy prices are a bit higher than the sell prices; the difference between the buy/sell is called bid/ask spread.

If you are selling a stock, you'll get the bid price; if you are buying a stock, you'll get the ask price. If you're buying a stock, it will cost more than you would get if you had the same stock and you were selling. The difference between the two prices, the spread, is pocketed by the dealers and floor brokers as their profit for the service of being market makers. Financial products that are traded in massive quantities daily usually have a tight spread: the difference between the buying and selling price is very small, or tight.

For example, if you were to buy one hundred shares of Apple stock (AAPL) at $101.50 per share and instantly sold all one hundred of those AAPL shares, your sales price would be about $101.40. You would instantly lose ten cents per share, for a total loss of $10 on the trade. This difference in price is the amount that the dealer or floor broker makes on the trade. Remember, the floor brokers make money with *every* buy and sell order that comes across their order book—it doesn't matter if you lost money on the trade. Each trading day, there are thousands of buy and sell orders, and the floor brokers earn a small sliver of profit on each trade they handle for their clients.

The volume at which shares or other financial products are traded is referred to as their liquidity. The more liquid a product is (i.e., the more often it is traded), the less the spread. The more illiquid a product is (i.e., the less it is traded), the wider the spread.

Bid/Ask Spreads Vary Widely

Spreads can vary widely between traded products: the spread of an electronically traded futures contract for 100 ounces of gold could be as little as $10. At the same time, the spread of 100 ounces of actual gold bullion from a reputable precious metals dealer could be as high as $30 per ounce, or $3,000.

PRIMARY AND SECONDARY MARKETS

Two other terms you'll hear as you learn more about trading are *primary market* and *secondary market*. The primary market is where new stocks and bonds are first made available for public purchase. When a company is raising cash for operations for the first time, investors can pay cash for an equity ownership stake in the company, which is embodied in shares of stock. In return, the owners of the company give up a percentage of control of their company to the investors. The company then takes the cash and uses the money to grow further. This initial sale of stock is called an initial public offering, or IPO.

Once the stock has been sold, it becomes a part of the secondary market, where it can be traded among investors and day traders with very few or no restrictions. Most times this is done through a brokerage account or an online trading platform. As a day trader, the financial products you will be trading will all be offered on the secondary market—you will be day trading by buying and selling on the exchanges through your brokerage trading platform. Your trading platform will differ depending upon the product you trade, whether it's stocks, foreign exchange, or futures. Not only are these different products, but each brokerage firm will offer its own. The basics will all be the same though: order entry, notations as to available purchasing limits, and each gain and or loss of every trade. The displays range from the very simple to the complex. Some professional traders use up to eight full computer screens at once: some for order entry, others for charting and market-related information.

The money paid for a trade is given to the previous owner of the stock, and the purchasing trader receives the stock. The company that originally issued the stock never receives any money from the secondary market. The only time the company receives the money from the sale of stock is when it's initially sold on the primary market. From then on, traders and investors buy and sell stock from their own accounts, and only to each other.

WHO'S WHO IN THE MARKETPLACE

Banks, Hedge Funds, and Trading Houses

Before you start searching the market, looking for trades, and living the often thrilling life of a day trader, it's best to know a little something about the institutions that are integral to the world's stock, currency, and commodities markets.

INVESTMENT BANKS

Within the world's marketplace of stocks, bonds, mutual funds, futures, and currency, there are a few key players. The first of these is the investment banks. These are at the top of the food chain in the trading business. This is because when companies are raising capital for the first time, it is the investment banks that write and prepare the documents, provide advice, and help "place" the initial run of stock that the company will offer. ("Place" in this context means the first listing of the stock on the stock exchange ever, thereafter available to the public to buy in their trading accounts for investment or trading.) As discussed earlier, if the company is raising capital on the stock exchanges for the first time, the first shares of stock sold to the public are called an IPO, or initial public offering. These IPOs are very complex. The company will hire an investment bank to determine how many shares will be sold, at what price, and if any other legal contracts will be tied to the shares. The bank will then use its vast connections in the investment world to find buyers of the stock at the initial price. This is the price it will sell at when the company goes public.

Investment banks have first dibs on the stock and will sell large blocks to their best customers. Many times regular traders can own shares of the new stock after it has debuted on the exchange and is therefore trading live.

HEDGE FUNDS

The second group of players in the markets is hedge funds. These are privately owned trading houses that invest both their owner's monies and their customer's monies at highly leveraged amounts. Not only are hedge funds highly leveraged pools of investment money, but they also use several different trading styles as well. These range from higher-level views of the world's trading environments (such as Global Macro funds), which trade any financial product with a "no restraints" policy on where gains can be captured, to derivative-only funds (managed futures funds) that are designed to make money when stocks go up or down in value (long/short funds), or even special situations funds (leveraged buyouts, or distressed asset funds, which only buy stocks in companies that are undergoing trauma: management takeovers, bankruptcies, fiscal trouble, etc.

Hedge Funds and Regulation

One reason hedge funds are attractive to investors is that they're less regulated by the SEC than many other financial institutions. However, in the wake of several significant scandals such as accusations at SAC Capital in 2010 of insider trading, that situation has begun to change, and there are more attempts by government agencies to oversee hedge funds.

These hedge funds can be massive buyers and sellers in the finance world. They sometimes use both equity and derivative positions to diversify their accounts to a very sophisticated level. These days, most hedge funds also use computer modeling and statistical programs to help determine and capture the best trades with the least trading risk. Overall, hedge funds are managed by the most sophisticated and powerful day traders and position traders in today's world markets. They play often and big. Hedge fund buying and selling can move the markets up or down. People take notice when a rumor of a large hedge fund making a trade is in the news. This is because most hedge funds are very secretive in nature—not only are their inner workings and methods kept quiet, but the fund managers keep a low profile as well—which only adds to the mystique of working for or investing in them.

Hedge Fund Performance

The major wealth management firms heavily recommend hedge funds of all investment styles. Some houses such as UBS and Morgan Stanley recommend that 15–20 percent of an investment portfolio should be invested in alternative investments for proper diversification and risk/reward profile. Of this 15–20 percent, hedge funds are included along with other forms of complex alternative investments, such as private equity and derivative funds.

Hedge fund performance has gone up and down over the years; they generally do best when the world's stock markets and economies are in turmoil. They are designed to offer maximum diversification to an overall investment portfolio and are built with layers of diversification. If the equity markets of the world are all doing well and European, US, and Asian markets are doing well, then traders and investors will most likely earn more and do better with a unidirectional, nondiversified trading strategy. In this market condition, stocks will generally move in one direction most of the time. While there may be up-and-down days, on average the market will move in one direction over weeks and months (or even years!).

In other words, economies that have great stock markets are great for day trading. Not only that, but simpler trading strategies work the best. Unidirectional and nondiversified, long-only equities or equity futures can be the best and highest performing trading strategies. Keep it simple! Buy low, sell high. If the market seems to go up every day, then go long only (buy low and sell higher). This is easy to understand and simple to set up on your trading platform. Currently the markets are conducive to simplified trading strategies. Another thing to remember is that simple long-only trades are cheaper to execute than diversified trades due to commission costs.

PROFESSIONAL TRADING HOUSES

The third type of investor (aside from independent traders) is professional trading houses, such as mutual funds and investment companies. Mutual funds are pools of monies that are professionally managed by fund managers. These investment vehicles are generally long-only equity or bond funds.

If you have a 401(k) at work, you are most likely investing in professionally managed mutual funds offered by mutual fund families. These mutual fund families offer customers professionally managed investments with smaller minimums and excellent diversification. Mutual funds pool their customers' investments. They then take the money and buy stocks or bonds (or both) with great diversification. These mutual funds can hold ten, fifty, or a hundred or more different equity positions of different amounts. The managers will then buy and sell, capturing short-term gains for their shareholders. Shareholders will also capture gains on stocks or bonds that go up in value in the market, even if they haven't been sold yet (these are referred to as unrealized gains). Investment companies such as mutual fund families are one of the largest buyers of equities and bonds in the marketplace due to the vast number of investors—especially retirees—using them.

COMMONLY TRADED PRODUCTS

Different People Trade Different Things

Before you begin day trading, you'll need to know some of the different investment products that can be traded. Some of them are easier to understand and set up as trades but offer less potential for return. Other products require a more complex trade setup but offer more potential to trade at higher returns.

TRADING STOCKS

The most basic type of day trading is trading equities also known as stocks. This is because the basic concept underlying this type of trading—i.e., buy low and sell high—is easy to understand, and online trading platforms such as E-Trade, Merrill Edge, and Scottrade make it simple. Stock trading works well when the world's stock markets are generally going up in value and when the economy is good.

Go Long, Go Short

If you buy a stock expecting that its price will rise, you're taking a *long* position. If you sell a stock in the expectation that its price will fall and you'll be able to buy it back at a lower price, you're taking a *short* position, or *shorting* the stock.

Equity Order Entry

When you're day trading stock, you sign in to your trading platform and type in the symbol of the stock (such as Apple Inc., with a symbol of AAPL). On most trading platforms it will show the current price of one share, along with the maximum number of shares you can afford to buy with the money currently in your account.

The next step is to enter the number of shares (say, ten shares), and then click the "Buy Now" button. Instantly, your trade is entered. You now own ten shares of Apple. If one share of Apple is selling at $100 per share, your total cost of the ten shares is $1,000 ($100/share × 10 shares). The trade has a small additional cost, usually under $10 (in this case, most likely around $5). Your trading platform now shows that you own ten shares of AAPL, with a true cost of $1,005.

Stock Symbols

The website *MarketWatch* (www.marketwatch.com) has a handy service that allows you to look up stock symbols. Just type in the name of the company and you'll find the stock symbol, the current price of the stock, its previous closing price, and other helpful information.

Monitoring Profits

If Apple stock goes up in value, the trading platform will show your trade value moving from $1,005 to a higher figure as each share gains value. If, as the minutes and hours tick by, the price of AAPL goes from $100/share to $102.50/share, your AAPL trade will show a value of $1,025 ($102.50 × $10 shares). Because you've spent $5 to buy the shares of Apple, the trading platform will show the net profit of the trade at $20. As you can see, in one day your trade has turned a $20 profit, or made a 2 percent return for the day.

As we said earlier, day traders close their trades at the end of the day. If they do their job well, they realize a profit and end the day with cash in hand. Closing out your trade will cost you an additional trading fee, typically a flat rate of around $5 for this type of trade. If the Apple trade was the only one you made during the day, this would leave you with a $15 profit. While this $15/trade seems small, it is a trade with very little risk or effort. You're in and out in a few minutes or hours, and your cash is back in your account, safe and sound.

If you made this or a similar trade each trading day, you'd net $225 in profits per month on your $1,000 trading account. This is 22.5 percent profit per month, or about 250 percent per year return on your $1,000 account. These types of trades are safe and manageable, and in this case your trading account would grow to $2,500 by the end of the year with very little effort.

As the amount of money in your account increases, you can also take on bigger and bigger trades, increasing your profits even more. This type of trading could easily and safely return 250–375 percent on a $1,000 account.

LEVERAGED EXCHANGE-TRADED FUNDS

Now let's see what happens if you up your game and engage in more complex trading. This involves using leveraged exchange-traded funds (ETFs).

An ETF is a basket of multiple stocks that can be traded on the markets. An ETF trades at a specific dollar amount but contains fractional shares of twenty to fifty different stocks, each valued at a fraction of their current trading list price. An ETF's trading value is determined by adding the dollar amount of the pooled assets and dividing that by the number of shares outstanding (that is, the shares available for traders to buy and sell). ETFs are favored by professional traders in part because of the benefits that come with diversification (the multiple company stocks contained within the fund). ETFs also often have massive trading volumes, which can result in significant daily gains. This makes them perfect for day trading.

Derivatives

Here's another useful term in this discussion: *derivatives*. If you were reading the papers during the 2008 financial crisis, you probably came across this word a lot. A derivative is a financial contract or asset whose price is determined by the price of something else. For instance, you want to buy a commodity—say, bushels of corn—as an investment, hoping that the price of corn will go up. But you don't want to store a thousand bushels of corn in your garage. You can instead buy a futures contract, which specifies that at some determined point to come, you'll take delivery of that corn. If the price of corn goes up, so will the price of the futures contract, which you can then sell to someone else for a profit. The futures contract is an example of a derivative.

Leveraged ETFs are the same as ETFs but they are financially engineered to use margins and derivatives in such a way to amplify the movement of the same base ETF by either two times (2x) or three times (3x) the gain. In other words, a base ETF might move up 1.5 percent during the trading day, while the 2x ETF would move up two times the same amount, or 3 percent. The same for the 3x ETF: it would move up 4.5 percent. It should be noted that while 2x and 3x ETFs offer higher gains, they're also riskier and more expensive than ordinary ETFs.

Bull and Bear ETFs

Leveraged ETFs also come in "bull" and "bear" designs. A bear refers to a *bear market* (when the markets are falling) and a bull refers to a *bull market* (when the markets are going up). A bull ETF 3x would go up three times the percentage of a normal ETF, while a bear ETF 3x would make money when the normal ETF goes down.

Bear ETFs can be complicated to use, but they do offer the day trader a simple method to set up trades that make money when the market is falling. The best way to use these is intraday, meaning they are traded within a single trading day during normal market hours and not set up before the market opens. As you will learn later, while still trading in and out during one day, it is possible to program a trade before the markets officially open in the morning and still close out the trade before the ending of the day. In this case, you wouldn't want to use bull and bear ETFs with pre-programed trades. The key is to get in and out quickly: ride the 2x or 3x bear for profit and then sell to lock in your gains. Bear ETFs are risky, so you should be cautious and only use them to make a little extra profit in bad markets.

MORE COMMONLY TRADED PRODUCTS

Futures and Foreign Exchange Trading

Two other markets that lend themselves well to day trading are futures and currency trading (referred to as Forex), though they are a bit trickier to trade than stocks and ETFs. Futures contracts are easily shorted (which means the day trader will make money when the market goes down) and Forex trading relies on one currency going up or down against another currency in order for the trade to earn a profit.

FUTURES

A futures contract, in essence, is an agreement to buy or sell something in the future at an agreed-upon price. As discussed earlier, futures are part of the group of financial products called derivatives.

The exchanges determine the number of units and settlement date of futures contracts, and they can't be modified. This means that contracts are uniformly interchangeable, so trading is simplified. Each futures contract has a buyer and a seller. One of the parties involved in the trade is a hedger and one is a speculator. The hedger enters into the contract to offset her risk that the future price of the product will move up or down against her.

For example, a manager of an airline gets the feeling that the price of jet fuel will go up substantially in the next six months, and this price increase will make it difficult for her company to make a profit. She buys an oil future with a set price for oil six months in the future to lock in the price of jet fuel for her fleet of airplanes. The set price she locks in is one that she knows her company can afford to pay for fuel and still make an acceptable profit. With the contract she is hedging her fuel expense risk; in other words, she is managing the future expenses and profit of the company.

Hedgers

A hedger is someone who uses the physical product he's buying or selling. He uses the futures trading contract to lock in his price and minimize his losses when he finally either buys or sells the commodity sometime in the future.

At the other end of her oil future contract is a speculator. This speculator does not have an actual need for oil or jet fuel. He does, however, think that the price of oil will be less than the contract price in the next six months. Seeing an opportunity to make a profit, he buys the futures contract that the airline company manager is selling. The speculator makes money on the futures contract when the locked-in price of the contract is less than the actual price of the commodity—in this case, oil. For example, if you buy a crude oil contract for one thousand barrels at $70 a barrel in July for oil to be delivered in November and the actual price of crude oil increases during that period, the value of your futures contract will also increase. If oil moves up to $90 per barrel by the time the contract expires, you own one thousand barrels of oil at $70 per barrel, which you can sell on the market for $90 per barrel, making a profit of $20,000 ($20 × 1,000 barrels). Futures contracts like these are bought and sold in huge quantities daily, creating a profitable market for day traders.

Standard & Poor's

The Standard & Poor's 500 Index (S&P 500) is a market indicator based on five hundred of the largest companies listed on the New York Stock Exchange (NYSE). It's used as one of the key indicators for the overall health of the stock market.

Margin and Futures

Futures contracts offer a margin up to 50:1 (in other words, for every one unit of collateral you put up, you can borrow fifty times as much). This means if you used full margin on your futures account, you could theoretically amplify the gains of the S&P 500 Index of 1 percent up to fifty times more, or 50 percent gains. This is the maximum amount of the trading value of the account. To manage the risk in your account, you might only commit 20 percent of your total portfolio to the trade, meaning you would earn about 10 percent gain on the trade. To explain further, if you used 20 percent of your total portfolio at 50:1 margin, it would look like this: .20 × 50 = 10 percent. Therefore, you would earn 10 percent gain on each actual 1 percent gain made by the future.

As you can see, the higher margin of futures allows you to amplify your trades at a much higher rate than you could with stocks or ETF trades. You can make large trades in a futures brokerage account, much larger than you can with a stock brokerage account. A $2,500 cash balance in a futures account allows for $125,000 worth of S&P 500 futures contracts, for example, whereas a stock trading account with the same $2,500 cash balance only buys $3,750 worth of S&P 500 ETFs.

Futures contracts are a bit more complex due to the rapid fluctuation of trade values and the constant account monitoring that they require. It takes skill to make trades at a 50:1 margin. All the skills you'll learn in this book—reading the market, studying the news, tracking the world's economies, and looking for good trade setups—will be tested to the maximum with futures trading. It is not for the faint of heart, but it is where the professionals can earn a big living. The profits can be huge: 100 percent or more gains in trading accounts monthly are common. At the same time, many futures traders find them quite difficult to master and close their accounts within a few years of struggling and racking up losses.

If you're sure you've mastered the basics of day trading and more advanced techniques, then by all means move on to futures trading. The markets are the same: gold, oil, and the S&P 500 are the largest and easiest futures markets to master and trade in. They offer direct connections to the ETF and equity world, allowing for great on-the-job training. It's possible to trade agricultural futures contracts such as corn and soybeans, but these are difficult to trade because their prices follow grain demands, weather, and international trading contracts, as opposed to strictly economic news.

S&P 500 Futures Contracts

In the case of the Standard & Poor's 500 (S&P 500) Index, each contract acts as a dollar representation of the whole S&P 500 Index. In other words, if the S&P 500 Index lists a value of 2,575 points, a futures contract for the S&P 500 will trade at $2,575.

Day trading this futures contract allows you to gain in the fluctuations of the index (in which movements of 0.5–1.5 percent daily are common) but at a much more leveraged rate than you would be able to with an S&P 500 Index ETF. Take, for example, the ETF designated by the symbol IVV (iShares S&P 500 ETF). If you were to trade the S&P 500 Index ETF IVV and you used a full 50 percent margin in your account, you could amplify a 1 percent gain in the index by an additional 50 percent, making it into a 1.5 percent gain—which is not too bad for a trading day.

Points

The points value in an index is an arbitrary number calculated by the values of the stocks, multiplied by a special and complex weighing system used to represent each company's dollar value relative to each other.

CURRENCY TRADING

In currency trading, or Forex (foreign exchange) trading, the trader picks two currencies and decides which currency will gain in value against the other. If you go to Europe and exchange your US dollars for euros, you are, in a sense, going into the Forex market; you're "selling" US dollars (USD) and "buying" euros (EUR). If many people, traders, banks, and governments sell one currency and buy another, this pushes down the price of the sold currency and boosts the price of the bought currency. In the stock market, if everyone is selling AAPL, then the price will go down. The same principle of supply and demand applies to currency trading.

Forex trading is easier than futures trading. While there are a variety of margins available—10:1, 20:1, 50:1—there are only a small handful of currency pairs that are available on most Forex trading platforms. From these, a day trader can master two or three currency pairs and do very well for herself.

Trading the same two or three currency pairs over and over, day in and day out can make a Forex trader an expert quickly. This expertise naturally leads to better and more successful trading, and therefore higher profits. You should consider currency trading as a way to have large, profitable trades (20:1 and 50:1 margin) that you can master in a relatively short time. Your account size can be small too—a $250–$500 cash balance in a Forex account is more than enough to get you started and make substantial profits quickly. It's normal to see $50–$75 daily profits in a $500 Forex account, and the trading can be done twenty-four hours a day, nearly six days a week. In short, for the day trader just starting out, Forex is the place to be. Forex is the perfect combination of trading power and easy mastery.

Currency Value

Besides supply and demand, a currency can rise or fall for a number of different reasons. These can include inflation (which makes each unit of currency worth less), political instability, rising or declining productivity, and natural disasters. Effectively day trading in the Forex market means becoming a student of international political, social, and economic conditions.

TRADING BASICS

Know Day Trading from the Ground Up

Most people who are in the stock market, bond market, or other type of investment are really investors and not traders. What makes the difference between investing and trading in the market? The real answer is twofold: leverage and time of trade.

TRADERS

Most traders use leverage in their accounts, either by using margin accounts or trading leveraged investment vehicles (such as leveraged 2x or 3x ETFs or leveraged mutual funds). In either case, the account is designed to use the dollar balance of the account plus any invested assets as a down payment for a loan from the brokerage house to borrow more money and then invest more with this borrowed money.

For instance, a trader has a $5,000 balance in his account, consisting of cash or stock (or mutual funds). Based on this, the brokerage house will "lend" him more cash using the balance in the account as collateral for the "loan." The trader will then use a combination of his cash and his available loan to make purchases of securities beyond what he could have bought with his cash. Securities can be purchased in excess of 150–175 percent of the cash balance of the account, depending upon the quality of the collateral.

If you are to use margin, then the higher the quality of your collateral, the higher the limit of additional margin the brokerage firm will allow. In the case of volatile stocks or leveraged ETFs, your brokerage firm might be limited to only 50 percent additional margin of your total account value. Higher-quality assets in the account always allow a higher level of margin, up to the amount specified by regulation.

In times of low market volatility and better economic times, government regulators allow the brokerage houses to increase the available margin, which offers traders larger trades overall. The looser margin rules often come during an economic environment of low interest rates, the benefit of which is then passed on to the trader. Remember, the margin is a loan, and prevailing interest rates apply to the trader's margin—which in turn is a cost of trading and can eat into the profitably of the trade!

Margin Rates May Vary

Regulators set the margin leverage amounts available to traders according to the health of the markets: in good times, leverage could be as high as 90 percent, but in bad economic times they could drop to as low as 30 percent or less.

INVESTORS

Investors usually have cash-only balances in their accounts. Many of these account holders have their retirement money invested in financial securities, either in their 401(k)s at work or in an IRA or Roth IRA at a brokerage firm. The money is designed to be used at some specific time in the future, and the date is usually known, since most people know more or less when they're going to retire. Investors put money in the account in a lump sum and then use it to buy securities, which they then hold for months, years, or longer. Alternatively, they could put cash into their account at timed intervals, such as when money is deducted from each payroll check, month after month, year after year, and placed in a retirement account such as a company 401(k).

Buy and Hold

The investor's philosophy is usually "buy and hold," meaning that the investment will see higher returns if the stock, bond, or mutual fund is *not* traded but rather held for extended periods. The idea is that the markets go up steadily over time and that there is no benefit to selling in short time frames.

Often, an investor will also reduce risk through a strategy called dollar cost averaging. The investor puts away the same amount of money into his chosen investment at set intervals, usually with each paycheck. This is the method that is used in payroll deduction for 401(k)s and self-directed IRAs. This method works especially well with long-term investment goals such as retirement needs or children's college tuition funding programs. And if the market takes a sudden downturn, the entire fund is not impacted—just that part that's already invested.

TRADER VERSUS INVESTOR

To sum up:

Traders

- Use leverage as much as they can to amplify the gains of their trading accounts with added purchasing power through margin accounts
- Use this margin, which is actually a loan issued by the brokerage house, to purchase more stock

- Are in and out of a trade in a matter of minutes, hours, or days; occasionally, a trader will hold a position for a few weeks or a few months (called position trading)

Investors
- Almost exclusively use cash accounts with no leverage
- Only use the cash on hand in their accounts to buy stocks, bonds, mutual funds, or other securities, and will rarely borrow to buy more
- Are into their purchases for the long haul
- Use the dollar cost averaging method to buy into the same security at regular times, regardless of price (for example on the fifteenth and thirtieth of every month)

It's the Taxman!

Brokerage house financial advisors are trained to give advice that allows the owner of the account to hold the securities for as long as possible, if for no other reason than to minimize taxes. Remember: a stock or security that is sold within one year is a short-term gain and is taxed at a higher bracket. Investors are usually more "tax conscious" and would like to avoid paying higher taxes.

Chapter 2

Creating a Trading Plan

Developing a good trading plan is much like making plans to go on vacation. You wouldn't show up at the airport without booking your tickets and knowing the flight schedule. And you certainly wouldn't fly to a distant city without having your hotel room booked and reserved. Trading is much like that: you do best if you've planned your buys, profit points, and sell levels. You also do best knowing how to exit a trade that is going bad or, better yet, knowing when to exit a bad trade before it turns into a significant loss.

A GOOD DAY IN THE MARKETS

An Early Evening, Looking Over the Markets

Let's take a look at what a good day for a day trader is like. Good days can be lazy or exciting, but they always come with good profits.

It's Sunday night, about six p.m. Central time, and you're cleaning up the kitchen after dinner with the family. You're watching cable television's Bloomberg Asia, which covers the earliest of the markets to open, along with the equities, Forex, and economic news.

SCANNING THE NEWS

While the television is on, you scan the upcoming economic reports. Your full-service broker, UBS, sent you a report late Friday night, which covered all of the week's upcoming world economic news release dates. You notice that the European Central Bank is meeting on Wednesday; you also notice that UBS is predicting a 0.25 percent increase in interest rates across Europe. The next thing you observe on the UBS report is that China's economic outlook is getting stronger, and with the Chinese government set to make a statement on Tuesday, things are looking good for the world stock markets. You look at economic reports that are upcoming for the week and make note of the other economic and political news and how it will affect the markets.

THE BEGINNING OF A TRADING SETUP

Somewhere between dinner and cleaning up, there is news that OPEC has made a surprise announcement about oil production cuts. Oil's been at $43 a barrel for three weeks, and you have a short on

West Texas Intermediate (WTI) with a short e-mini oil futures trade, thinking it will go lower. (The e-mini oil is a US-based futures contract that tracks the price of West Texas Intermediate oil prices but is priced for a five-hundred-barrel contract value, as opposed to the full-sized contract of one thousand barrels.) "Wow," you think, "this is going to shake up the commodities market." The futures markets are already open in the US, and you quickly rush over to your desktop and close out your short WTI oil trade. Other traders around the world are monitoring the news too, and the oil contract you were in is starting to rise in price, which would have turned your short trade into a loss.

Since the oil story is sure to be big news on Monday morning, you analyze what trades you could set up. Your goal is a few well-diversified overnight trades that you could close out in the morning when the US traders are up and trading full blast.

GETTING YOUR TRADES PLACED

First things first: you switch up the short futures trade to a smaller long oil futures trade. Instead of five e-mini contracts on short, you go for two futures contracts, but this time they're long, set to profit when oil goes up in value.

Thinking you'd like to diversify the trade as much as possible, you switch your trading platform to the Forex (currency trading). At 50:1 leverage, you set up a nice 10,000 USD short EUR/NOK currency trade that costs you $200 of your margin account. You know this short EUR/NOK trade will show a profit when the Norwegian krone gains value against the euro. This is actually a subtler trade than the oil futures, as Norway is a major producer and exporter of crude oil to mainland Europe. Since you've been trading in the Forex market for almost a year, you know that higher oil prices will also mean a higher value for the Norwegian krone versus the euro. This is a nice, subtle, yet highly leveraged trade setup that in the past has paid well.

To capture the higher oil prices even further, you place a trade of a "2x long" leveraged oil company stock ETF on your stock brokerage trading platform. While the US markets won't be open until tomorrow morning, you put the trade in anyway and set it for "At the Open." This means it will fire off the trade in the first seconds the market opens. You're unsure of the price, but you know it will only rise during the day—in fact, you're planning to close out this trade at the end of the trading day, after all the news stations have reported the news to US investors. Investors follow news too, and you know they'll be calling into their brokers and buying stock in oil-producing companies throughout the day.

HEDGING YOUR TRADES

When your profit-capturing trades are set up, you call your best friend, who's also a day trader. She's watching the news too. After a laugh about all the money you guys are going to make, you discuss the best way to hedge the profit trades as cheaply and easily as possible. You both decide the best way to hedge out the long oil commodity trade is with a short commodity trade. Using your Forex account, you short the Australian dollar (AUD)/USD trade for $15,000. The short AUD/USD Forex trade will make money when the Australian dollar loses value against the US dollar. This is a cheap hedge, because at 50:1 leverage, it's going to cost only $300 worth of your margin account.

Lastly, you put in a stop-loss order, which is designed to limit the losses in this trade if oil goes up quickly and all other commodities-related products follow suit and go up in value. This trade will work when commodities such as nickel, iron, and gold go up in value on the world market, as commodities often all go up in value at the same time. Remember: different commodities are different products. Grains and foodstuffs would naturally go up if the crops were bad due to poor weather during the growing season. Oil would go up if there was a hurricane in the Gulf of Mexico, as this is where much of the US gets its crude oil from. And gold would go up if markets were falling, or worse, if geopolitical problems such as terrorist attacks or military action upset the world as a whole. Finally, the short AUD/USD Forex trade will make money if the world's markets get spooked and equities markets worldwide fall in value. This happens because the world's markets are generally "risk-on" or "risk-off."

If it is a risk-on day for the markets around the world, the world's currencies that pay higher interest (i.e., countries with high economic growth) are also considered to be a risk-on trade, and then would gain in value against the currency of a country with lower economic growth, such as the US dollar, Japanese yen, or the Swiss franc. These countries are more economically established and therefore have lower growth rates than high growth economies. Generally, the growth economies are the developing nations such as Brazil, the currencies of southeastern Asia, and the currencies of some eastern European developing nations (such as the Czech koruna, Hungarian forint, etc.). At the same time, the currencies from countries that are known as "commodity currencies" (i.e., the country produces and exports commodities as its main trade good) will also be considered a risk-on currency. This is due to the fact that the economic well-being of developing nations is tied to the overall well-being of the world economy (but they are growing at a faster pace than the established countries) and the commodity-producing economies are reliant on a strong world economy to ensure the constant demand for the goods they produce, such as oil, copper, iron ore, etc. The idea is:

if the world's economies keep growing, there will be more and more demand for the commodities, as they will be used up in the many manufacturing processes across the globe. On the other hand, if the world's economies slow down, manufacturing will also slow, lessening demand, lowering prices, and finally causing a slowdown in the countries that produce those raw materials.

What's a Hedge?

Traders use the word *hedge* a lot. Essentially, it's a trade you make to offset possible loss from another trade. Think of it as a kind of insurance.

The ten o'clock news is on, and your trades are set. You're set to make money in the oil market overnight and close out your trades in the morning at a profit. You've also set up your well-thought-out trades to hedge out some of the risk in your account, with the added risk management technique of an automatic closeout of the hedges if the losses are too great when they move opposite of your long oil profit trades. Dishes are done, kids are in bed, and trades are in: it's going to be a profitable day in the markets tomorrow.

A BAD DAY IN THE MARKETS

Keeping Calm and Cool

Most of your trading days will be structured, controlled, and profitable. While your aim is always to anticipate your trades and map out your profits, some days are filled with bad news. These days can be disasters to your profits and can be nerve-wracking to go through. Here's an example of what it's like during one of the market's bad days.

YOUR OVERNIGHT TRADES ARE SET

You've had a run of good days lately, but today it's different. You've read the market and you see that there is a risk—on sentiment in the market. Basically the rule is this: the market comes in two forms, risk-on or risk-off. You'll know it's a risk-on day when the stock market is up, your long trades are doing well, and the people on the news channels such as CNBC are excited in a positive way. All is good in the market, there is nothing to worry about, and everyone seems to be getting rich. You'll know it's a risk-off day when the markets are down by large amounts (over 1 percent), everything on your trading screen is in "the red" (it's green when going up and red when going down in value), and when you tune into CNBC or your favorite website for financial news and the stories are negative: all the commentators are predicting the end of good times and are openly wondering, "Is everyone losing money? Is everyone going broke?"

The market and the public are very fickle: there can be a few days of the market being risk-on, and then a few days of the market being risk-off for no apparent reason.

You've placed your risk on long AUD/CHF (Swiss francs) and long EUR/CHF trades, along with some well-thought-out automatic profit-taking stops. Going to bed, you realize that you're going to wake up with a bit of profit, feel good about the day, and go to work with a little extra money in your trading account.

THE BAD NEWS STARTS ROLLING IN

You get up, make your coffee, and begin making breakfast with CNBC on in the background. There is a lot of news chatter about foreign exchange rates and an intervention of the Swiss National Bank in the market. *What?* you think. Turning up the volume, you realize that the Swiss National Bank has intervened in the currency market and drastically changed the exchange rate between the Swiss franc and other world currencies. The markets have reacted with turmoil overnight. Basically, the Swiss have forced the change in exchange rates after having them locked in for years. The EUR/CHF has gone from 1.10 to .98 in seconds overnight, meaning the Swiss franc has gained against the euro drastically. This has wiped out every short Swiss franc trade worldwide, yours included. Your trade was set to make money when the euro got stronger against the Swiss franc, but the opposite has happened. Now the question is just how badly the trade has affected your account.

You know bank interventions such as this are rare and can cause massive damage to an account. You look at your chart. There is a huge spike at three a.m. when the bank moved the rate. You look at the balance in your account. The FX platform has tried to hold on to your stops, but the huge number of trades worldwide that were shorting the CHF has caused the Forex broker to cause your trades to "slip" and fall before it could "stop you out" (i.e., trigger the automatic closing orders you preprogrammed to avoid losing too much on a trade). Your account slipped because of the sheer number of losing trades worldwide, and the broker's computers couldn't handle all the automatic stop-out trades firing off at the same time (when this happens, it can be a big problem!). The good thing is your trades got closed before your account totally lost out. The bad thing is, the slippage in the account caused such a delay in the stop-exit trade (the one you set up to prevent major losses) that you lost 40 percent of your account value within seconds. The trade closed out, but you're stuck with the deep loss on the trade.

Shaking, you realize it could have been very bad for you in your trading account. You close the computer and go through the motions of getting ready for the workday. *Good thing I have a regular job,* you think, while the newscasters on CNBC excitedly talk about the overnight currency markets. Quickly, you evaluate the rest of your positions. The long oil mini future trade is up 0.5 percent in early trading along with your long e-mini S&P 500 futures trade, as it is still a "risk-on day" with worldwide assets, but your e-mini gold futures is down. That's okay, because you knew that this was to be your hedge against the larger risk on trades, and you have the overall big hedge for your monies in the Goldman Sachs Macro Strategies Hedge Fund ETF (symbol: GVIP); this is an ETF that is built to closely follow the Goldman Sachs Hedge Fund VIP Index, a widely used hedge fund value index.

ASSESSING THE FINANCIAL DAMAGE IN YOUR ACCOUNT

Overall, you realize that your account was properly hedged with the long gold futures hedge (which would go up if the markets got bad overall as a worldwide safe haven trade), and you also have the macro hedge with the hedge fund ETF. Both of these positions have helped your account immensely: the losses haven't been that bad, as they've been properly hedged to prevent too much of a loss from one trade.

What's a Macro Hedge?

A macro hedge is a trading style that incorporates all the world's financial products and markets—gold, currencies, bonds, commodities, worldwide equities, etc.—into one balanced, *internally hedged* product, where you can trade one ETF to hedge your portfolio, while within that ETF there is a deeper, internal level of hedging going on: diversification within diversification.

You look further, and you realize it is still a risk-on day in the markets—you read it right—but the Swiss National Bank's interventions couldn't be predicted. While the currency account is down 40 percent, you've managed to hedge out enough risk so that the overall net value of your account is only down by 5 percent. Not too bad. After a little quick math you see that you're actually okay for the day, but the whole thing has really shaken you. You know there is only one thing to do on days like this: close out all your trades and go 100 percent cash. Get out of the markets and cool off. It was a bad day for you and others worldwide, and there could be some massive sell-offs or risk-unwinding coming in the next few weeks and you'd really like to sit it out. No more trading for you for a while.

Quietly, you close out all of your trades, one by one. You do this manually, with the click of a button, even though the trades look like they will be going up for the rest of the morning and you have the chance of earning more on each trade and erasing some more of your overall losses. The fact is, you and the rest of the traders worldwide are a bit shaken from the overnight news, and they are thinking the same thing: get out now while the getting is good, and wait for the markets to sort it out. You know markets are all intertwined and that the Swiss franc is heavily used to finance trading and commerce worldwide. You're thinking it could get really messy while it is sorted out, and you'd like to lessen your risk overall. By closing out your account to 100 percent cash, you can earn some interest while resting easy, waiting for this news to get factored into the world's markets.

WRITING A BUSINESS PLAN

Treat Day Trading Like a Business

One of the best ways to look at day trading is to think of it like a business. You will need a computer, iPad, or smartphone. You'll also need an investment of cash in your trading account. The good news is that you won't need a big cash outlay to start, and you can have a lot of fun with even the smallest trading account.

HOW MUCH YOU'LL NEED TO DAY TRADE

Your investment in day trading can be as small as a few hundred dollars if you are trading in the currency markets and $1,000 if you are trading in the stock market.

Futures trading is a bit more complex—most minimum accounts are of $2,000, but due to the way the margin is settled daily, it would be best to have $2,500 or more in your account before trading. If this amount isn't in your futures account, you run the risk of getting intraday margin calls daily whenever your trading account falls below the $2,000 threshold.

What's a Margin Call?

A margin call is when the broker or exchange declares that cash must be added to your account to bring it back up to a predetermined cash balance. If you don't do this, the trades in your account will be automatically closed out. Since this can be very unprofitable, it's best to keep your futures account well above the minimum before trading.

KEEPING TRACK OF YOUR EXPENSES, GAINS, AND LOSSES

Because day trading is a business, you should keep track of your expenses such as Internet, phone, and if you have a home office, part of your mortgage or rent. You should also track the cost of subscriptions to trading magazines and newspapers. All of these expenses should appear on your profit and loss statements.

Taxes

Day trading profits are considered short-term capital gains and are therefore reported as regular income on personal tax returns. When you're successful at day trading, these gains and profit can add up quickly, amounting to hundreds or thousands of dollars a year in profits. The gains you make trading will be taxed at your regular tax rate. If you're already in a high tax bracket, the profits you make in your trading account will be taxed at this rate. This means you'll need to build in tax expenses into your trade gains along with your trading expenses ($5–$10 each into and out of your trades).

The best way to handle any kind of taxable business is to keep track of all your expenses. You can even link a debit card to the cash balance in your brokerage account. Think of it this way: you could deposit $5,000 in your stock trading account and get a debit card tied to the cash balance. A good plan would be to trade all month, booking all profits and absorbing any losses. At the end of the month your account would be higher in value than when you started. You could then take a small amount out of the account to cover the expenses associated with trading, pay those bills with the money, and leave the rest in the account to multiply and compound for the next month's trades. Your second option would be to take out the small amount to cover your expenses, along with a set "salary" or fixed cut of your trading profits. Your trading expenses would be paid, and your "salary" would go to living a better life, paying household bills, etc. You'd leave some profit in your account to build over time.

TAKING YOUR PROFITS AND TAKING A SALARY

As we said earlier, day trading should be treated like a business. The recommended approach is to take a set salary on top of your expenses, just like a paycheck from a job. This method ensures you are enjoying the profits of your day trading business.

It's generally not good to "hoard profits" by allowing your account to grow and grow without taking out any money. Larger and larger trades are glamorous to be sure, but they can be difficult to manage. If the economy turns bad and if the stock market and Forex markets get rocky, you might enter into difficult trading times. It's at these times that you'll be glad that you used and enjoyed some of the profits you accumulated by trading: car payments, dinners out, vacations, college tuition, etc. Good traders know to not get greedy—greed leads to poor trading decisions and risky behavior. Staying hungry with day trading can lead to safer, more profitable trading.

THE POWER OF KNOWING YOUR PROFIT GOALS

When you're starting out, it's good to think about what you'd like to accomplish with your day trading. What would you like to do with the money? Seems silly, but that's really the best thing to ask yourself. If you have a goal, you can work toward it. If you'd like to make enough to pay for a new car payment, and you need $400 a month in extra income, then you know you'll only need to trade enough to earn this much. After your first $400 each month, you know you can stop aggressively trading since you've reached your goal. You can slow up and look for only the best trades with the least amount of risk. You can get into only the best trades and make a little more with little risk. You can also sit on the cash, patiently waiting for the next month, when you'll be at it again. This way you'll be keeping the risk profile of your account to an absolute minimum while you earn your car money, just like a job.

The business plan can help you with your risk profile and trading frequency. You can trade as little or as much as you want, starting and ending each day with cash. It's a good business and you can find it quite profitable and enjoyable.

MAKING THE BEST USE OF YOUR TIME

How to Plan Your Trading Day

You can start your day by listening to the business news stations, such as CNBC or Bloomberg, while you get ready for the morning. They often offer some very good insight as to what economic reports are scheduled to happen later on in the day. This serves as a good way to get into day trading early, before some of the markets open. A review of the markets can help you recognize some very profitable trading opportunities that are coming along during the day.

EARLY MORNINGS WITH THE MARKET NEWS

Reviewing the news can also alert you if the markets are in a state of unrest. This unrest may be due to what happened overnight in the Asian or European markets, or the fact that a big US economic report is coming out. Here's a typical scenario:

You wake up at five a.m., start the coffeemaker, read the Markets section of *The Wall Street Journal*, and casually watch the morning news shows. You note that overnight the markets in Germany and London were in disarray, and at two p.m. this afternoon, the US Federal Reserve will make an announcement on interest rates. Armed with this information, you could decide that it is in your best interest to take the day off from active day trading. If you do, though, you'll miss out on any upside from potential positive news made during the day. As well, you'll insulate yourself from any whipsawing or wild swings back and forth in the markets preceding and following major news. You have to determine whether those two possible upsides are better than risking your account on a big news day.

These types of unpredictable market days are best handled by trading in your practice account, or demo account. The demo account is the account that your broker will give you to practice trading ideas with "play money." They might fund your account with $25,000 worth of digital play money that isn't really cash. You'd be able to log in, scout for trade setups, set stop losses, and get to know your profit points. You can even execute orders with the same live pricing that a real account would see and use, all the while using and risking only the play money in your account. Any wins or gains throughout the day would be "play wins." At the same time, on really difficult trading days, and when it's best not to risk real money, these demo accounts can serve as a great testing and learning environment for you to try new trading scenarios in a real market setting.

Chapter 3

The Cost of Trading

While the profits and benefits from day trading can be considerable, there are some down sides to working on your own within the markets, trading your money day in and day out. Trading is like no other business where money is the product: if you have a bad day at work, you still get paid; no money is at risk. With trading, though, you are putting money at risk, and each trade carries a possibility of loss. In this chapter we'll look at the costs of day trading—both financial and human.

WORKING ALONE

The Loneliness of Day Trading

After you determine that you can temper your emotion, know your risk tolerance, and have disposable cash to trade with, the question remains if you can work alone. Day traders often trade in an office in their homes, away from the business and financial districts of their hometowns or nearby cities. You might find that you miss the interaction of coworkers, the friendly chats with other commuters on the train going to work, or even the act of walking down to the corner coffee shop with an office friend for a much-needed afternoon break.

Not only does this mean that you will not have coworkers to speak with about things such as last night's game, but you will also not be able to discuss your trading ideas with an office mate. You might even find yourself wishing that you could approach a manager or boss about a trade you are about to make involving more than the usual amount of your money. In these cases you might find it comforting to have a superior to help shoulder the burden of your decisions. However, that's not part of day trading. All the cash, knowledge, skill, and risk-taking are yours and only yours. While it might be easy to think of the benefits of day trading and working on your own (and there are many!), you should consider if the business is right for your temperament. Here are some of the issues to consider when working alone as a day trader, both bad and good:

Working Alone As a Day Trader
- There is no one checking your attendance.
- There is no one to make sure you are at your desk for the opening bell.

- There is no accounting department to record your gains and losses.
- There is no technical department to fix your software/computer.
- There is no one to delegate to: printing, faxing, filing, or running out for sandwiches.
- There is no such thing as a paid sick day.
- There is no need for nice clothes to wear to the office.

Like most day traders, you will probably decide that working alone isn't that bad. In fact, the list of benefits that come from successfully day trading goes far and beyond the bad issues that you might encounter. Most of the real issues associated with working alone relate to your ownership of your trading account and your trades. You are the only one who makes the decisions about your day trading career and your account. The only performance review will be your own satisfaction that you are building up your account (and net worth) through your day trading efforts.

Thinking of your day trading as a business applies here as well:

- Show up for work at regularly scheduled times.
- Wear your "work clothes" if this gives you a more professional attitude, as this might make you feel like you are on the clock.
- Give yourself periodic reviews of your trading activity.
- Schedule vacations with family or friends at regular times throughout the year, just like you do with a normal job.
- Create a routine, both for starting and ending your day.
- Stay in touch with people; just walking to the neighborhood coffee shop or the market can lead to refreshing contact with other people.

THE DAY TRADER'S TOOLS: TRADE LIKE A PRO

The Day Trader's Tools

TAKE CARE OF YOUR TOOLS

Look at trading as a job and your trading account as your tools. A mechanic would be excited when a customer brought in a Ferrari to be worked on, but he would perform the tune-up with a cool professionalism that is apart from his love of Italian cars. He would not abuse his wrenches or gauges in such a way as to diminish their value or harm them—or the car—in any way. This is a good way to start to think about trading and your trading account. You will be working on very expensive, exotic things while using your precious tools of the trade—i.e., you will trade a particular sector using your precious trading account.

KEEP A COOL HEAD

This idea of trading as a professional and treating trading like a business is one of the key elements to a successful long-term day trading career. Your emotions will be tied to every trade before it is made, but you don't have to let them overwhelm you. You can learn to use a cool head to plan entry points (the point at which you make your initial purchase of a stock, commodity, or currency), as well as using calm, calculated feelings to execute an exit from a trade to capture profits. There are many stories of day traders feeling elated with their unrealized gains on a trade (unrealized means the profits are still "on paper" and not yet in the day trader's account, as the trade has not been closed out yet) and not being emotionally able to exit the trade in hopes of yet more gains.

Trades Gone Bad

There are always stories of trades going bad and the profits lost. Day traders often say they "should have taken the profits," and "what was I thinking?" If you can learn how to manage your emotions about trading, you can be on your way to making money on good trading days and keeping your money on bad trading days. In day trading, good emotion management is the key to good money management.

TIME COMMITMENT

The second thing to consider before you begin your day trading career is if you can make the time commitment. Depending on how much you already know about markets, it can take anywhere from one month to several seasons to get enough general knowledge to begin successfully trading. At the minimum you must commit yourself to a structured study period for a few weeks to get acquainted with the markets. You do this by reading books and magazines designed for independent day traders, as well as skimming through the daily business newspapers such as *The Wall Street Journal* and *The Financial Times*.

Often, people want to start placing trades and making profits immediately. If you want to be as successful as possible, it's best to take your time to learn the markets before committing any amount of money. There are stories of people opening an account online in a matter of minutes, depositing money, and hurrying to trade. There are also stories of day traders placing trades in fresh accounts when they aren't even sure how to use the trade input screens. They make trades in the wrong direction and for the wrong amount. Such disasters can be avoided by taking your time while opening an account, learning how to operate it, and learning what you would like to trade.

Once you are in full swing, you'll find time speeding by as you sit in front of your computer, trying to capture the gains of the market as it moves up and down. While some markets can be traded into the evening and overnight, most of them are open only during the mornings and early afternoons. This means that in order to day trade, you must be available to follow news, read charts, and place trades during these hours. It is possible, however, to trade part time. Some trades can be made on Sunday afternoons and after work during the week. If you would like to begin your day trading on a part-time basis, then this is a good option for you. Just allow yourself enough time to learn the market on your shortened schedule.

AVAILABLE CASH

For any job, some equipment is usually required. If you are a plumber, you might need a van to haul your plumbing equipment. If you are a painter, you might need brushes and ladders. If you are an accountant, you might need computers and tax software. When you are a day trader, your equipment is your trading account. It's usually filled with a combination of cash and margin. Just as a plumber needs a certain size van, you will need a certain amount of money to begin day trading.

When you're just starting out, you can do well with a small amount of cash. You can have a lot of fun and learn a lot with as little as $250 in your account. For example, if you have $250 in your foreign exchange trading account, you could spend the night making small, quick trades while watching television. It is possible to do this each night and make enough money to pay for your breakfast doughnut, lunch, and afternoon coffee all on the profits you make from the night before. This can actually be a really good way to get used to the market lingo, software, and the process of order entry all while building a positive trading experience.

TRADING WITH SMALLER ACCOUNTS CAN BE REALLY REWARDING

It can be a really rewarding experience to begin trading with smaller amounts. Sometimes, though, having a smaller account can tempt you into foolish behavior. You may argue that because you have a smaller dollar amount in your trading account you should make high-risk/reward trades. After all, even if they go wrong, you won't lose that much money. Resist this thinking. Improper position size, margin mismanagement, and a series of misplaced trades can lead to losses that can close out your account.

If you start small and get used to the feeling of winning a trade you planned, you can gradually add to your account and trade larger and larger amounts. You will, however, need to have enough discretionary money from your normal household budget to use for trading. It is not wise to trade with your rent or car payment money. You should trade with money that is earmarked for your trading account—i.e., it should be money that you are able to lose or at least use for a risky venture such as day trading. After you are up and running as a full-time professional day trader, you will be able to make biweekly or monthly withdrawals from your account as a salary draw. Until then, the money you use to trade should be allowed to grow with each winning trade.

BROKERAGE BASICS

Choosing a Brokerage Firm

Before you begin your day trading career you will have to choose a brokerage firm. Think of this selection process much like an interview for a job vacancy you have at your day trading firm. There are the basic interview questions to ask, including can the broker do the job and does he have the skills to succeed. Lastly, you need to know if the candidate is a good "fit" with your day trading company.

TYPES OF FIRMS

When choosing a brokerage firm you will have different options, depending upon the type of sector you are interested in and your opening balance.

BROKERAGE FIRMS		
Type	**Benefit**	**Disadvantage**
Deep-discount online firms	Good for stock and ETFs	Not broker assisted
FX brokerage firms	Low account minimums, high margin	Not broker assisted
Multisector	Low-to-mid account minimum, high margin	Not broker assisted
Combination firms	Broker assistance, multiple sectors	High minimums
Full-service firms	Excellent source of trading information, broker assistance for setting up complex trades, multiple sectors	High minimums, high transaction costs

Discount Firm

The first type of brokerage firm you can consider is the deep-discount firm, which only offers services online. These brokerages will offer a discount on the price if you exceed a certain number of trades, usually fifty in a month. If you plan to do Forex trading, be ready for a completely hands-off approach from the brokerage firm. Many do not offer any broker assistance and often offer only limited technical assistance, if any at all.

FX Brokerage Accounts

If you plan to day trade in an FX account, you will need to keep good records of your cash deposits, cash withdrawals, and all the gains and losses for each trading day. These firms will not send you a statement every month and will not list the trades you make over the quarter or year. Most likely they will keep track of your overall profit and loss as it accumulates in your account, but often this will roll over from year to year. Considering this, with the FX accounts and others that do not send you a statement or send you a loosely based one, it is best to keep track of your profits, losses, and interest earned on a daily profit and loss sheet.

Foreign currency brokers usually charge low commissions on popular pairs, called majors. Higher commissions are charged on other currency pairs, or crosses, consisting of two major currencies that are less commonly paired. The highest commissions are charged on infrequently traded pairs, referred to as exotics. These are any of the pairs that involve the developing countries (even if the other currency is a major FX such as the EUR or USD). Examples of this include the US dollar/Brazil real (USD/BRL), the Euro/Czech koruna (EUR/CZK), and the Euro/Hungarian forint (EUR/HUF).

The pairs may also include some of the developing nations of Asia. The more infrequently an exotic is traded, the more expensive it can become. On the other hand, the cheapest FX pair to trade is always the EUR/USD, as this is the most heavily traded currency pair in the world. Since the costs of the commissions and brokerage fees are subtracted from your overall profit, it makes sense to try to get the lowest fees possible for each round trip of trading. Some commissions are a flat rate, with larger amounts, and effectively will put you at a loss even before you start to trade.

FX Pricing and Pips

FX brokerage accounts set their pricing in a different way than a typical stock brokerage account. They usually have a set percentage of the currency amount of the currency pairs posted in their commission structure. The commission is deducted automatically from your trade balance after the trade is placed. This has the net effect of putting you at a loss at the moment of the trade. The commission is based upon hundredths of a percent, often referred to as basis points. These basis points commissions are called pips—i.e., each basis point is a pip. The pip price that you pay for your trade will stay the same regardless of the size of the trade. In other words, if the commission structure for a EUR/USD trade is 1 pip and you place a trade of 10,000 EUR/USD, the commission will be 1 EUR for the round trip of the trade. If you place a trade for 1 million EUR/USD, the commission will be 100 EUR for one complete opening and closing of the trade. The charge will be taken out at the time of the trade; on the other hand, if you traded stocks or ETFs, you would be charged for buying and then again when you sold. Each time you buy and sell is a separate cost.

Multisector Brokerage Firms

The lack of records provided by a brokerage firm should not prevent you from considering whether it fits your needs in other matters. Perhaps you would like to be able to trade gold, oil, and FX; in that case, you would do well by opening up a multisector account. Multisector brokerage accounts usually have a higher minimum then the pure FX accounts, as the *lot size* or smallest trade size in the other sectors might require a higher minimum account cash balance to trade effectively. For example, some brokerage firms offer full multisector accounts with 200:1 margin with an opening deposit of $2,500. Again, with this type of account you would not get any type of broker assistance in setting up trades, and you would not get any type of statement from the firm. You can keep track of your daily net gains, losses, and interest earned using preprinted paper trading forms. These forms also have places to record the stock index levels and overall market conditions present during that day. They can be used for tax purposes and to have a permanent record of your trading successes.

Combination Brokerage Firms

Combination brokerage firms have licensed brokers available to assist in setting up trades and hedge trades. They have two types of pricing structures: one for online trading at the discount rate, and one for broker-assisted trades at a higher, full-service rate. This higher rate can be worth the price if you are just starting out, setting up a complicated trade, or would just like to "talk through" the logic of a trade before making a commitment to it.

Full-Service Brokerage Accounts

Going through a full-service brokerage firm will help greatly if you're planning to invest, even though the high commissions will prevent you from day trading in this type of account. The research and education supplements provided by full-service firms are indispensable in your day trading career. They offer overall market analysis, sector and industry-specific analysis, and information regarding the trading potential of the S&P 500, ETFs, commodities, and currencies.

Although most brokerage firms will give you access to some kind of news feeds and research reports, some of the reports are nothing more than a collection of articles that are available on public access news sites. The key is to get access to the best research and day trading ideas that you can, even if you have to pay for it. The way around this is to open an account at a full-service brokerage firm that offers insight into the markets you are trading in. Perhaps you can put your "other" money into this account—i.e., roll over your 401(k), open an IRA, or set up a retail brokerage account with your investments, long-term money, or mortgage. In this case you would use the full-service brokerage firm for your long-term investment (not day trading) money. You could then have access to the wonderful brokerage reports, research, and daily market, Forex, and commodities reports they publish. You could have an account at one of these firms and subscribe to their email list for their daily reports. These reports are usually well written and geared toward the institutional investor, offering daily in-depth analyses and recommendations, providing an essential tool for the active day trader.

The yearly price the full-service brokerage firms charge to keep the account open can be anywhere from $75–$250, but the benefits of having access to all their reports and information are worth the price.

STANDARD ACCOUNTS

Standard accounts usually only allow you to trade stocks and ETFs. These accounts do not allow trading on margin, meaning you will only have the buying power of your cash balance. Standard accounts are good for beginners, because the lack of a margin limits position size and risk. Additionally, you will be limited to long-only trades, a trade in which the stock or ETF gains in value when its price goes up.

FUNDING YOUR BROKERAGE ACCOUNT

Some brokers require account liquidations to be the exact method of account funding. In other words, if you put money into your account by check, wire, credit card, or PayPal, it will have to be liquidated in the same way. The money will have to come in and out using the same method. This is important when you are planning to make biweekly or monthly withdrawals from your account as a salary draw.

Your bank may charge a fee for sending funds to your account via federal wire; check with them about this. Fees for outgoing wires can range anywhere from $35–$75 per wire. Outgoing wires are usually only processed at the beginning of the day, Monday through Friday. This account funding method will work especially well if you are sending larger amounts, as the fees associated with the wire are fixed regardless of the fund amount, acting as a volume discount. With a bank-to-bank "fed wire" (money that is sent from account to account through the Federal System Clearing House) a deposit is considered "good funds," meaning you can trade with them at the moment of the deposit without waiting for them to clear through the Federal System Clearing House.

The slowest method of all is to send a check. This traditional method costs only the price of a postage stamp and can be a happy medium between the cost associated with wires and alternative funding methods such as PayPal and debit cards. You will have to plan when and how much you will be sending, as it will take until the check arrives and clears before you can trade with those funds.

Chapter 4

Getting Started in the Marketplace

You've learned a bit about the markets, trading and day trading. Next you'll need to learn where is a good place to start: what to trade, how to look for good trades that will be profitable, and ways to get as much training as you can entering and exiting trades, as well as searching for trades that work to get the safest and easiest profits.

TRADING STOCKS

A Good Place to Start

Before you begin to day trade, you must determine what you would like to trade. There are several sectors of good products to choose from. The first sector we'll consider is stocks. Stocks are a good place to start because it is easy to understand what exactly is going to be traded.

STOCKS: PIECES OF A COMPANY

Stocks are representations of the net worth of a public company. Every public company divides its value into a certain number of pieces, or shares. Each share represents part ownership in that particular company. A share of XYZ Company is the legal equivalent of part ownership of every desk, truck, building, and piece of property on XYZ's balance sheet.

Caps

Stocks are divided into groups depending upon their market cap. The market cap is the number of shares outstanding in the market multiplied by the price of the share. For example, if XYZ Company has one million shares outstanding and each share of XYZ stock is $10, the market cap of XYZ is $10 million or 1,000,000 × $10.

If a trader thinks a stock is cheap, she will buy it, and if a different trader thinks of the stock as expensive, he will sell it. A stock's price will move up and down as it is bought and sold, as if it is caught in a constant tug-of-war. This action creates an opportunity for you as the day trader to ride the movements up and down, piggyback-style, capturing profits as you move in and out of the trades.

The Pros and the Cons of Day Trading Stocks

One of the benefits of day trading stocks is that they are easy to research. Almost all brokerages offering day trading capabilities allow access to high-quality, in-house research that you can cross-check with the research put out by independent firms. Trading individual stocks also offers the opportunity for large percentage movements (2–5 percent or more per day) when a stock is in play. A stock (or other investment) is in play when some news has come out that concerns the company and the news has caused other traders to take notice.

An example is when a large retail chain reports earnings: let's say the analysts and traders have anticipated the company did really well the previous quarter (such as during the holiday season) but when the chain makes the official profit announcements, it is only half of what everyone expected. This is terrible news for the stock, and it tumbles like a rock falling into a ravine. Not only is this news terrible for that stock, but all other retailers in the same or similar market sector that sold the same type of product are now under huge selling pressure, as the traders expect similar profit and sales figures from all similar retail stores. In this way when other traders take notice, a stock will go up or down, depending on whether the news is perceived as good or bad for the company.

A downside of day trading individual stocks is the tendency of traders to develop a trading portfolio of undiversified positions, which leads to a concentration of risk. Think of the "don't put too many of your eggs in one basket" adage. While large concentrations in very few positions (i.e., being undiversified) might lead to large losses (or gains!), it doesn't always. Sometimes a stock in your trading portfolio can be "stuck in the mud" and fall out of other traders' sights, leading to stagnant trading days. Your money could be tied up in a stock that doesn't move enough to make a profitable trade, while putting that amount of your tradable cash or margin at risk of being a bad trade.

A second drawback of day trading stocks is that your margin is greatly limited as compared to FX or futures. Think of margin as a revolving credit card with which to day trade. There are regulations as to the amount of margin (or credit) you can use for different sectors. Some sectors, such as stocks, are limited to around 50 percent of your total account including all stock and cash positions.

EXCHANGE-TRADED FUNDS

We discussed exchange-traded funds (ETFs) a bit earlier, but now we're going to talk about them in more detail. ETFs are "baskets" of individual stocks or other underlying products. They are subject to the same valuation procedures as individual stocks, but they offer the diversification function of a mutual fund. The mutual fund–like property of ETFs can be a real advantage, as the diversified basket reduces the concentration risk of individual stocks. At the same time, when you day trade ETFs you can capture the price movements of an entire industry sector such as financial company stocks, oil company stocks, or technology/biotechnology stocks. Certain sectors are in play at different times and are influenced by different factors. With this in mind, day trading ETFs can offer a very neat, compact, and effective way to trade a whole sector when that sector is moving rapidly and in play.

Flexibility in Trading ETFs

You can use an ETF to day trade almost any type of position you can imagine. There are even ETFs that offer a "short" position, allowing you to make money when an ETF's basket of stocks goes down in value. These ETFs are often called bears.

The Pros and Cons of Day Trading ETFs

Some of the good things about day trading ETFs include diversification, multisector availability, and their popularity with traders and institutional investors. The latter can lead to relative safety and overall good day trading opportunities. The few disadvantages to day trading ETFs are limited to the fact that your trading margin will be restricted to the same amount as individual stocks, as ETFs are traded on the same exchanges as most individual stocks and are regulated as such.

DAY TRADING FOREIGN EXCHANGE

Dealing in Currency

After you gain experience in the relatively simple world of individual stocks and ETFs, you may want to enter the world of day trading foreign exchange, gold, commodities, and futures. These sectors can allow a day trader to amplify each trade, as the allowable margin ratios can be quite large, and in some cases unbelievably so.

WHAT SETS FOREIGN EXCHANGE APART

Day trading in the foreign exchange (FX) market has become one of the preferred areas for traders looking to make a living at trading. It is an unregulated market, open around the world, trading twenty-four hours a day from Sunday afternoon to Friday afternoon.

Trading FX differs from other types of trading in a variety of ways. The first difference is what is being traded: as opposed to companies, baskets of companies, or a commodity, what you are trading is the difference between the exchange rates of two currencies. For example, you could place trades on the supposition that the Australian dollar will strengthen against the Japanese yen (AUD/JPY), the US dollar will strengthen against the Swiss franc (USD/CHF), or the Norwegian krone will get stronger against the euro (NOK/EUR). You sell, or short, the currency you think will go down and use the money to buy, or long, the currency you think will go up.

ADVANTAGES TO DAY TRADING FX

One benefit of day trading FX is the low minimum account openings. Some brokerages allow you to open with $25 and some as low as $1. How can trades with such low amounts be made effectively? It's because FX margin ratios can be anywhere from 10:1 to as much as 500:1 in some European- and Asian-based Forex brokers. That means you could trade $50,000 worth of currency with only $100 in your account. As you can see, there is a lot of money to be made even with small account balances.

Also, due to the limited amount of currency pairs available because there are only about fifteen currencies that have enough volume for FX brokers to offer for trading (EUR/USD, AUD/JPY, CAD/USD, etc.), there is a lot less to study and learn, and you can quickly get a feel for the market. It's relatively easy to analyze trends in the FX market when you're looking for trading ideas. FX lends itself well to both economic and news analysis as well as technical chart trends. Traders look to the economic reports published by the major world central banks to value the currency pairs. Also, the study of technical charts can easily show when a currency pair is stretched and due for a correction.

Some currency pairs such as AUD/JPY are classically known as measures of a stock trader's risk appetite and move in tandem with the world's stock markets. When the world's traders feel they want to accept more risk into their portfolios and buy more stock, the high-yielding, risky Australian dollar will also appreciate against the lower-yielding, safer Japanese yen.

Quantitative Easing

Central banks are very aware of when their country's currency gets over- or undervalued in relation to its main trading partners. Banks can, and often do, intervene in the currency markets to force the adjustment of their currency. This is called quantitative easing, and it can cause rapid movements in the nation's currency. Quantitative easing can create a wonderful day trading opportunity, because a whole country's financial reserves are working to move the markets.

THE DIFFICULTIES OF FX DAY TRADING

FX day trading does have its downside, though. The fact that things can happen quickly and unpredictably is a negative aspect of FX trading that is shared with other sectors. FX markets are subject to unpredictable impacts, such as economic and geopolitical news like unemployment figures, military skirmishes, and other unexpected events. Other news and events influencing the FX market are sudden (or not so sudden) central bank interest rate changes. For example, a Pacific Rim currency such as the Australian dollar (AUD) can increase its interest rates overnight while you sleep, causing a long-lasting "jump" in the value of the currency against a lower-yielding currency such as the Swiss franc (CHF). This could cause serious problems with any short AUD/CHF positions you might have been holding overnight with thoughts that the safe-haven Swiss franc would appreciate against the high-yielding Australian dollar.

One More Thing about Day Trading FX

A factor that works both for and against you when day trading FX is the availability of such large margin amounts. Once you get used to the amount of leverage in your FX account and learn how to use it safely, it can be a very effective tool to amplify your profits. If used excessively, however, it can lead to large losses quickly.

GOLD AS A CURRENCY

If you are thinking that the FX market might be a good place to trade, you might also consider the gold market. Day trading gold is unique, because you have to think of it as both a commodity and a currency.

You might be thinking that it is easy to see that gold is a commodity, as it has the physical property of a metal. But why is gold a currency? This is because the price of gold moves inversely with the value of paper money such as the US dollar, the British pound, and the euro. While there is a relatively fixed amount of gold, there is an ever- changing amount of printed and electronic money available. When there is more money in circulation, the price of gold goes up because there is more money bidding on the same amount of gold.

Study the potential for gold trading beginning in the early fall to get a feel for where the gold market will be heading—usually up! This is because physical gold is heavily purchased and given as gifts during the Indian marriage season in the fall and the Chinese New Year in the spring.

Gold and Inflation

Day trading gold can be like day trading the market's sentiment on inflation. The more the market thinks there is potential for inflation, the more traders will bid up the price of gold. The opposite is also true: the more rosy and positive the economic picture, the more traders will sell gold, causing the price to go down.

The Benefits of Day Trading Gold

Trading gold can be a bit simpler to decipher than other trading markets. It's easier to read the fundamentals of a potential trade when there are relatively few influencing factors. Also, a 400-ounce brick of gold (the size of the gold bars that are stored in the vaults at Fort Knox) will never go bankrupt. More than a few companies have lost a majority of their value through bankruptcy in the history of the stock market. This will never happen with gold. Gold has no balance sheet, no debt, and no product to sell. Also, there is a limited amount of gold, and it will most likely be in demand for some time.

The Problems with Day Trading Gold

Gold prices are subject to geopolitical as well as economic news, both of which can be fast coming and unannounced (with often illogical effects on the market). Another issue that affects gold's price is that gold is strategically bought and sold by the world's central banks. An announcement from a major central bank that it's buying or selling large quantities of gold could move the markets quickly and for the long term, with both good and bad effects depending on how you are positioned. Because of the limited amount of gold available to trade, both central banks and major institutional investors (such as hedge funds) can have a big influence on the price of gold in the market. Lastly, the nature of gold's day tradable products, mainly ETFs and futures, offer downsides themselves: low available margin for ETFs and high minimum account size for futures.

COMMODITIES

Raw Materials

Commodities are also known as raw materials or hard assets. They are a day trader's dream when there is a strong economy. Yes, they lost some of their steam after the banking crisis took hold in late 2008, but they remain traders' favorites for a variety of reasons.

EASY-TO-UNDERSTAND MOVEMENTS

Commodities are well liked because they have easy-to-understand reasons for price movement. Their prices are basically related to the world's economies. When the economies of the world are doing well, the prices of commodities usually go up. This upward trend can play out over days, seasons, and years. When commodities are in play, they are in play in a really big way. Following is a table of commodities, including the size of the smallest contract available, the exchange they are listed on, and the hours they are traded.

TYPES OF TRADABLE COMMODITIES			
Commodity	Contract Size	Exchange	Trading Hours
Corn	5,000 bushels	CBOT	9:30 a.m.–1:15 p.m. Central
Oats	5,000 bushels	CBOT	9:30 a.m.–1:15 p.m. Central
Soybeans	5,000 bushels	CBOT	9:30 a.m.–1:15 p.m. Central
Copper	25,000 pounds	CMX	8:10 a.m.–1 p.m. Eastern
Platinum	50 troy ounces	NYMEX	8:20 a.m.–1:05 p.m. Eastern
Silver	5,000 troy ounces	CMX	8:25 a.m.–1:25 p.m. Eastern

TYPES OF TRADABLE COMMODITIES			
Light sweet crude oil	1,000 barrels	NYMEX	10 a.m.–2:30 p.m. Eastern
Heating oil no. 2	42,000 gallons	NYMEX	10 a.m.–2:30 p.m. Eastern
Gasoline—NY unleaded	42,000 gallons	NYMEX	10:05 a.m.–2:30 p.m. Eastern
Natural gas	10,000 million BTUs	NYMEX	10 a.m.–2:30 p.m. Eastern

COMMODITIES AND THE WORLD'S ECONOMIES

Commodities can be an inflation trade, like gold, but they are more directly tied to the world economy's productions. In other words, it is not only inflation that pushes their prices higher. They gain when the world is in high production mode: building, expanding, manufacturing, and growing. This is because the goods and raw materials are the building blocks of manufactured goods (i.e., more steel is needed to manufacture more cars, more concrete for buildings and roads, more copper for electric wires in homes and buildings, etc.). Rapidly expanding countries such as China and India have a huge demand for raw materials when their economies are moving ahead strongly. With this in mind, commodities can have a unidirectional trend in good times. This means that while the price of oil and copper go up and down on a daily basis, the net trend over an economic period will generally be up for several years. This takes a little bit of the guess out of trading...just think net long (over time, an average of more long positions than short positions), and you will capture the slowly creeping trend to more and more expensive hard assets.

HARD ASSETS CAN BE UNCORRELATED TO THE STOCK MARKET

Hard assets can be relatively uncorrelated to the stock market. This means that commodities such as oil, corn, and copper have the potential to move independently of the stock market's everyday ups and downs. In this respect, knowing how to trade commodities can allow you to have a market to trade when traditional stock markets are trending sidewise, going nowhere, or otherwise stuck in the mud.

What Affects Commodities' Prices?

Commodities can have a great seasonal aspect. Gasoline gets expensive during the summer driving months, and natural gas and heating oil get expensive in the winter months. Day trading commodities such as grains and petroleum offers opportunities to capture profits related to unpredictable extreme weather, natural and manmade disasters, and geopolitical concerns. For example, heavy rains or drought in the Midwest can affect the price of live cattle, hogs, and grains, while orange juice usually goes up in price after an unusual cold snap in Florida.

Rapid, sudden movements in prices are a day trader's opportunity to make profits. When a commodity, ETF, or other tradable vehicle is in play, it is always possible to make money quickly. One trading day in May 2010, the stock market made a 9 percent plunge in a matter of hours. It recovered most of its losses by the end of the day, and the next Monday the S&P went up another 4 percent! If you entered the market in the bottom and got out of the market by the end of the day, you had a very profitable trading experience indeed. Some day traders were sweating it out, covering their positions to the downside; others were kicking themselves that they were away from the trading desk, shopping, traveling, or otherwise taking it easy that day.

MORE ABOUT COMMODITIES

Another thing you should think about when considering day trading commodities is this: although there are a few commodities ETFs to trade, most day trading in commodities is done in the futures markets. Trading commodities futures requires large account minimums, large amounts of leverage, and early-to-mid-day trading hours. If you are starting with a small amount of money or are building up your skills while keeping your full-time job, perhaps you should consider commodities after you have made the transition to day trading as your full-time career.

FUTURES

The Ultimate Paper Asset

When people say they trade futures, they mean they are trading fixed-size contracts that allow the holder to buy or sell an underlying product at a set price at a named date in the future. Futures specify the number of units per contract and a settlement date, both of which are set by the exchanges and can't be modified. This means that each contract for each type of commodity or stock future is set at the same amount. The only caveat is that there are full-sized and mini contracts: for example, a full-sized WTI oil contract is always for 1,000 barrels of oil, and a mini WTI oil contract is always for 500 barrels of oil. The same goes for wheat, corn, gold, silver, etc. contracts: they are always one preset size and can't be changed.

All like contracts are uniformly interchangeable. Each futures contract has a buyer and a seller. One of the parties involved in the trade is a hedger and one is a speculator. The hedger enters into the contract to offset her risk that the future price of the product will move up or down against her. The speculator is the pure trader, who has no need to enter into a trade to hedge his corn crop, fuel for his fleet of airplanes, etc. The speculator only trades for financial gain. The hedger or the speculator can be a buyer or seller: it is the nature of the purpose of the trade that determines if it is a hedge.

An Example of a Futures Trade

For example, a manager of an airline gets the feeling that the price of jet fuel will go up substantially in the next six months, and this price increase will make it difficult for her company to make a profit. She buys an oil future with a set price for oil six months in the future in an effort to lock in the price of jet fuel for her fleet of airplanes. The price she locks in is one that she knows her company can afford to pay for fuel and still make an acceptable profit. With the contract, she is hedging her fuel expense risk, as it is a form of managing the future expenses and profit of the company.

The other end of her oil future contract will be bought by a speculator. He does not have an actual need for oil or jet fuel. He does, however, think that the price of oil will be less in the next six months than the contract price. Seeing an opportunity to make a profit, he will sell the futures contract that the airline company manager is buying. Money is made on a futures contract when the locked-in price of the contract is less than the actual price of the commodity. For example, if you buy one crude oil contract in July for oil to be delivered in November at $70 a barrel, and the actual price of crude oil moves above the $70 contract price, the value of your futures contract will move in tandem to these price movements. If oil has moved to $90 by the time the contract expires, you own 1,000 barrels of oil that cost you $70 per barrel, which you can then turn around and sell for $90 per barrel. Your profit will be $20 × 1,000 barrels, or $20,000. These contracts are bought and sold in huge quantities daily, creating a very liquid and profitable market for day trading.

A RANGE OF PRODUCTS

Futures products range from commodities to financial products such as T-bill futures, foreign exchange futures, and S&P 500 futures. With their set contract size and delivery dates, they can be traded year round worldwide. The futures market is deep, with many institutional traders and companies coming together; it's also international. A Swiss food company might enter into a US dollar futures trade and offset it with the purchase of a wheat future. With this they can lock in the exchange rate from Swiss francs to US dollars and use the US dollars to purchase wheat to ship to their factory in Costa Rica.

T-Bills

A T-bill is a short-term debt instrument issued by the US government. They carry very low interest rates but are considered one of the safest investments possible. People, companies, and countries buy them to store their cash, much like a very short-term Certificate of Deposit at a local bank. It's possible to trade T-bill futures based on predictions of future interest rates.

ZERO-BASED FUTURES DAY TRADING

As a day trader you can trade futures using large amounts of margin, which can amplify your trading profits with each trade. Futures accounts are zero-based with profitable and losing trades being settled at the end of each trading day. This means losses will be subtracted from your account and placed in the winner's account, and the traders holding the losing end of your winning trades will add to your account. This will effectively decrease or increase your buying power the next day, so winning trades can be compounded by buying more contracts if there is a momentum to the market. This zero-based account settling coupled with high margin can lead to highly profitable trading days. In fact, futures day trading is sometimes the method that highly leveraged, fast-moving, technology-driven hedge funds use to capture very high returns.

Downsides of day trading futures include large account minimums and large contract sizes. Some of the financial futures contracts can be as large as $1 million per contract, which can be a barrier for even seasoned day traders. Additionally, the futures markets are usually opened in the mornings and closed by early afternoon. This would limit your ability to trade futures if you are building up skills while holding a full-time job.

STARTING TO TRADE

Information Sources and News Feeds

While there are many places to look for trading ideas, you should focus on two: trusted sources and market chatter. Trusted sources will tell you the most likely future direction of the market. Market chatter can be useful, but only after careful analysis.

TRUSTED SOURCES

These are usually the longer-term reports and market summaries that are published by your broker. Market reports and summaries offer a logical view of the market. They are often based on mathematics, past market activity, market fundamentals, and technical indicators. These longer reports should be read during times when you are not trading. You should study them for content and absorb the themes the analysts are presenting. For example, the report might say that there should be a "more cautious stance taken in the market overall for the next few weeks." You might learn that the S&P 500 has entered into an overbought range. This means that according to fundamentals, the stocks in it have an overall high average P/E (price/earnings ratio), meaning the prices of the stocks are too high compared to the estimated earnings of the companies. Also, the report might state that the S&P 500 has been sitting near a resistance level for a week, unable to breach an important level. Taken together, those two pieces of information tell you that the S&P 500 is near its top and will be there for a while. In fact, it might enter into a stall, or worse, a correction (when an overvalued market is sold off to more realistic levels).

You would know from this information that it is a good time to have a short position in the market—i.e., there's a good chance the market will move down in the next month and you would like to capture this movement.

Find the Right Firm

Brokerages are known to cater to either individual day traders or to institutional day traders. Firms focused on individual day traders will offer more explanations in their reports, both on the fundamental and technical sides. They have a more education-minded goal than the institutional-focused firms. Look for samples of a firm's reports to determine its bias.

MARKET CHATTER

The next place you can look for ideas is the short-term news reports, commonly called market chatter. Short-term news reports can be posted on stock market websites such as CNBC.com, MarketWatch.com, Bloomberg.com, etc., as well as the short-term news reports that take up the bulk of the news day on television news shows such as CNBC and Bloomberg. The key with short-term news reports is to use them to outsmart the markets. Remember, there are a lot of people reading the same reports and charts, and the market moves in a herd mentality. You will have to decide the point at which the price of the product is overbought, oversold, or neutral based on your overall knowledge and what the long-term reports tell you.

It's best to use short-term public indicators such as wire reports that provide buy and sell points to determine what most day traders are thinking. Again, reliability and accuracy of information is the key: use trusted sources only, such as those provided by a full-service broker or information news leads provided as a service with your trading account. There is a good chance that day traders everywhere have the same buy and sell points in their minds: they are all reading the same charts and short-term news reports. Because of this, never enter your trades based solely on the guidance of these reports. It is better to use them as tool to gather intelligence and to understand the thinking of other market participants. Would you listen to your auto mechanic discuss the time he had a concrete driveway poured and the contractor used the wrong mix? Would you use that as the basis of pouring your own concrete driveway? Wouldn't you be very selective of the sources of information in regard to your construction endeavors? This is how you have to think about the information out there regarding the economy, the stock market, oil, gold, interest rates, and currencies. People everywhere love to talk about money: they love to talk about how much they have, how much they don't have, the killing they made, and how much they lost in the market. Everyone has an opinion when it comes to money and the markets. But not all opinions are equal, and you shouldn't treat them as such.

Listening to the Market's Commentators

By their nature, news and Internet feeds have to have stories to fill the minutes and hours of the trading day. Even on the slowest, most uneventful trading days these news stations and Internet sites will deliver news with a heightened state of energy, which can make the information seem more important than it really is. Try to keep things in perspective.

GOOD OR EVIL: THE MARKET AND "NEWS DAYS"

Your first and foremost goal in day trading should be capital preservation. Your secondary goal is capital gains. This means that you should always view each trading day and each trade with the mindset that a cash position is the safest place to be and that you will only enter into a trade if there is a reasonable expectation of a capital gain. You should manage your risk to preserve your capital and only take measured risks in relation to the potential gain of a trade.

You should enter into trades with an understanding that the market will react and move in the future in a way that can be predicted with some degree of certainty. For example, you note that typically the S&P 500 trends in one direction for two to three days and then reverses. If the S&P 500 has been up dramatically for three days straight, then it and the other risk-sensitive trades will be ready for some of the market participants to sell off some of their holdings and engage in what is called profit taking. You also might have observed that when there has been a multiday run up in the market with big gains at the end of the week, traders will often relish their gains over the weekend and sell on Monday to lock in their good fortunes. With this in mind you could short the market, buy a bear S&P ETF, or build a position in risk-averse currencies.

When the primary goal of your account is to make capital gains, you will be forced to take risks with every trading situation. It would be unacceptable to sit out a day, and it wouldn't be acceptable to forgo a series of risky trades in favor of ending the day with nothing more than interest earned.

ECONOMIC NEWS DAYS

Economic reports are held in great secrecy before they are announced. Brokerage firms, television news commentaries, and

Internet forums will have predictions and statements as to what the market thinks the report will say. Often, when the economic report comes out and it is different from what the market expected, there will be a reaction: the market will move up or down according to how accurate the market predicted the news. On the other hand, if the report comes out and the market predicted it exactly right, the market often has already priced in what they expected. In other words, they built the expected positive or negative news into the value of their trades and positions. When this happens, the market will sell off anyway, as the event is in the past, everyone knows the actual numbers, and profit taking will take place.

Trading during the various days when the market is reacting to large amounts of positive or negative news and the world's traders are basing their mind-set of risk-on or risk-off trading on this good or bad news, and whether the news is from the United States, Europe, or Asia, can be very tricky; the outcomes can't be predicted with reasonable accuracy. Since capital preservation is your primary goal, you should avoid trading on news days. The markets will always be there; you can always trade after the news comes out. It is best not to have any positions in your account in the time leading up to the announcements, especially if the positions are directly related to the sector to which the news reports relate.

ADVICE ON TRADING IDEAS

Get Help When You Need It

There is an advantage to having some sort of assistance available when you need it. While the brokers at combination firms usually do not offer advice as to what to buy in order to make a profit, they can set a trade up for you that you might otherwise have trouble setting up yourself.

KNOWING WHEN TO GET TRADING ADVICE

For instance, suppose that the trading you are going to be doing for the next few days will tend to be "risk averse" in nature—e.g., you are going to be short in the S&P, long in gold, and long in the Japanese yen. Why would you make these trades? Well, if the market is risk averse, then you know the stock market will go down. Therefore, your short in the S&P will make money when the market goes down. As well, when the market is risk adverse, traders and investors world-wide will be selling their risky assets (stocks and high-interest/commodity currencies, etc.) and they will take the money from the sale and put it into "safe" assets. Safe assets are, among other things, government bonds, lower interest–paying currencies from developed nations (especially the Japanese yen, the US dollar, and the Swiss franc), and—the safest of all assets—gold.

In order to slow down some of the movement and dampen wild swings in your account, you could hedge against the risk-averse positioning in your trading portfolio. Your discount brokerage firm might switch into full-service mode and guide you; your broker might suggest a combination of small positions that would be structured to gain in value if the market started to take a riskier stance. Since the Swiss franc (CHF) is considered less risky (and moves up when there is less appetite for risk), the broker might place a short CHF position with a stop-loss order to prevent any dramatic loss in value to the downside. The positions will make money when the market goes down, and these two net positions have the potential to lessen the impact of a really big movement in prices in the wrong direction against you.

MORE TRADING IDEAS

Consider reading *The Wall Street Journal* in the morning before you begin to trade to get an idea of what the markets are doing. Switch to a monthly online magazine during your off days when you're not trading. You can polish your technical chart reading skills by reading *Active Trader Magazine* while spending time with your family in the park. You could even find yourself spending time listening to audio versions of the various periodicals and the on-air news magazines, podcasts such as *The Bulletin with UBS* (https://monocle.com/radio/shows/the-bulletin-with-ubs/), *Exchanges at Goldman Sachs* (www.goldmansachs.com/our-thinking/podcasts), or WBBM's (780 AM) *Noon Business Hour* (http://chicago.cbslocal.com/show/noon-business-hour). There are also downloadable online versions of *Moneytalk* (https://tunein.com/radio/Moneytalk-p20477/), a nationally syndicated on-air magazine devoted exclusively to the markets and money matters. You'll be surprised how much knowledge you can pick up in relation to the markets and economic matters, knowledge that can be directly tied to your day trading career.

DWELLING ON THE MARKETS

Dwelling on the markets and day trading will get you to the point that you are good at reading the markets, reading charts, placing trades, and making profits with your knowledge. If you are thinking about the level of the S&P 500, you might be wondering, *Why did it go up (or down) so much in the past week?* Or you might be thinking, *I have really made a lot day trading that S&P ETF. Why? Did I call it right, or did I get lucky? If I got lucky, should I stop trading and do more thinking about why I was in tune with the markets?* If you are trading oil you might start to dwell on where the market will be in the fall when the hurricane season starts. You might be thinking, *The summer was really cool. Does this mean the winter will be especially cold? If this is true, how should I be looking at heating oil and natural gas futures? Are the other traders thinking the same thing? Does my broker have any thoughts?*

If you are day trading FX, you could be thinking that the European Central Bank has been behind in raising interest rates in comparison to Norges Bank, the central bank of Norway. You should ask yourself, *Does this mean they might raise rates in the near future? Will going long on the EUR/NOK be a good trade after the European Central Bank makes its rate announcement later this month?* Or you might be shopping for a new SUV and notice that the new Volvo S90 seems really expensive. *Why? Is it time to go long on a Swedish krona trade versus the USD?*

Day trading what you like will go a long way in your studies and will get you to the point where you are naturally focused on the subject of the market, your account, and making money by day trading. Getting to know the ins and outs of the price of your trades is easier if you like the subject. If you travel to Europe, London, and Singapore, then it would naturally be easier to relate to the price of the currency as you are trading the FX pairs that contain them. Also, if you really like gold as an investment (which some people really, really do!) then you'll know the price of an ounce of gold day to day without any problem, as you will find it easy to relate to, and not just a trade you are making. Your goal is to get to the point that you think about your account all the time. This is how you will become an expert at day trading.

WHAT TO TRADE SEASONALLY

Changing Over the Year

Once you start to study the markets and begin trading, you will notice that during certain times of the year, different sectors have more volume and more volatility, both of which are contributions to a good day trading environment. You might even notice that some of the sectors have an overall unidirectional movement over a particular season, meaning the sector will trend on average in one direction for that season.

FALL AND WINTER: GOLD AND COMMODITY CURRENCIES

The trading year begins in the fall with the markets starting to gain volume, and there are more traders and gains. It gets more and more intense until it peaks, and then slows again around May. In fact, many professional traders all over the world take the summer off and don't trade at all.

During the fall to spring sessions is usually a good time to start to build overall long positions in the gold market, either using gold ETFs or gold futures. This is due to the fact that gold tends to build in price, starting with heavy physical gold buying in the fall and ending in the spring. You could also use long exposures to the commodity currencies such as AUD, CAD, and NZD to enhance your long gold positions. These currencies are called commodity currencies because they are the currencies of commodity-producing economies. For example, both Australia and Canada are heavy gold producers, and New Zealand is a major producer of soft commodities for Asia. Not all currencies are cyclical in nature, as most follow no seasonal trend.

Low Interest–Paying Currencies and High Interest–Paying Currencies

Lower-yielding currencies, such as CHF and JPY, are considered safer because their low interest rates indicate that they have less room to depreciate. On the other hand, the high-yielding currencies, such as NZD and AUD, charge a higher-risk premium: they have a greater distance to fall to come in par with the lower-yielding currencies.

FALL, WINTER, AND SPRING: EQUITY-SENSITIVE FX AND THE S&P

The stock markets tend to build interest after the end of the summer vacation months and volume in the month of October. With this in mind, you can make good trades with stocks, S&P 500 futures, and ETFs. Certain currency trades are subject to the stock market's ups and downs. If you are interested in trading the currency markets, you could go short on the US dollar versus the Swedish krona (USD/SEK) and go long on the Australian dollar versus the Japanese yen (AUD/JPY) and the New Zealand dollar versus the US dollar (NZD/USD). When the market is falling and there is overall risk aversion, a long exposure in the yen (JPY) or the Swiss franc (CHF) will usually result in gains, as traders flock to the lower-yielding (lower interest rates) currencies at this time. Historically, and lately, the JPY and the CHF are very low, if not the lowest interest rate currencies.

FALL AND SPRING: ENERGY

During the fall and spring seasons certain energy trades are in play. In the fall, with the onset of the cold winter months, the energy that is required to heat homes and offices can present good opportunities for trading. Natural gas futures, heating oil futures, and energy company stocks are good sectors to watch. In the spring and into the summer driving months, gasoline and crude oil futures and oil company stocks offer day trading opportunities.

WHEN TO TRADE THE HOT MARKET

The market usually just chugs along in a general, lazy upward motion with only the occasional downward movement. Then there are other times when a market—whether equities, a currency, a commodity, or an index—is on a roll and is moving full steam ahead. It is during these times that traders all over the world are on the same side of the trade, all trying to buy, and this pushes the price of the sector higher and higher with each day. A market such as this can only be described as a runaway train, as there is a lot of momentum behind it and it seems to move in only one direction with no end in sight.

When you are aware of this type of movement in a stock, sector, or index, you have two choices. The first is that you can get out of the way: the market is on a roll, is moving forward, and probably will not stop until a bubble is created. Eventually the bubble pops, sending the market back to premomentum levels. This is a defensive play and is a very safe way to not get caught up in the beginning of the creation of a problem in the market. Markets, sectors, and securities can only expand in price for so long, and when they reach the end of their growth, everyone wants out at the same time, causing a lessening in demand and eventual collapse in price.

The secret is to get into the security before the bubble collapses. This is known as getting into the hot market. Knowing when to get into the hot market is not as important as knowing when to get out. The peak is never quite signaled until it is too late and the sector has already started to collapse. In a hot market, the best thing is to keep your trades focused in a very short time frame and never have a trade on the books longer than one trading session. This means no overnight trades, no carry trades, and no longer-term, accumulation-type trades.

Trading Bubbles

Bubbles can happen in every market, sector, security, and with every form of goods. In the Netherlands during the seventeenth century, for example, there was a sudden craze for tulips. The price of these flowers soared until abruptly the bubble burst. Massive fortunes disappeared almost overnight. In the US during 2008–2009 we experienced the collapse of a bubble created by housing prices.

This should not cause any less returns, as a hot market moves in one direction rapidly almost every day, often over several months or even a few years. With this in mind, get in and get out with your trades, since you never want to be the last one in the trade as it starts to go down. When a hot market is in a correction stage, that sector should be completely off limits to trading. When the security is going down in price, don't be fooled into thinking that you are doing well and getting a value by buying on the dips as you would in a normal market. This type of market is often too choppy to navigate, or too difficult to predict, going down and then up again dramatically and unpredictably. Also, if the sector is falling, it can be really difficult to know where the bottom is, when it will change and go back up again, or when it will just sit there, stuck in the mud. Steer clear of these corrections! It's better to trade in your demo account at these times.

In a collapsing market there are no dips, only lower and lower prices. The sector should be off limits from day trading and position building for a while. This is true because as there are usually many people who made money on the upswing in the price of the sector, there are usually many more that got burned and lost much when the bubble burst. These people remember their pain well and will be reluctant to get back into that security again for a while—many will never return again. This does not preclude the fact that there are other sectors, securities, and objects to speculate.

KEEPING THINGS IN PERSPECTIVE

The Short-Term and Long-Term Views

When day trading, you will need to learn how to keep a short-term and long-term perspective. You will also need to learn how to use day trading software to get account information in relation to your open orders and your profits for the day. Finally, it is very beneficial if you can use a practice account. It will help you become adept at your order-entry skills and give you a place to try out new trading strategies and ideas.

SHORT-TERM AND LONG-TERM PERSPECTIVES

You should keep your analytical perspectives in two time buckets: short term and long term. Your short-term perspective should be ultra-short: the time it takes to evaluate the day's market conditions and news, look for setups, and commit to a trade. This short-term perspective will then last until the trade is closed out and reviewed. Things to look for when evaluating a trade include:

- Cash and margin amounts
- Initial and one-third sectional position sizes
- Price-of-entry points
- Overall risk level of the trade

Fifteen-second, thirty-second, and one-minute charts will help you get a short-term time frame perspective. Five-second charts will let you see each trade as the security moves up and down in the market, but do not show enough perspective of the overall market. These charts can be found on every trading platform, as they are the mainstay of all active day traders: therefore almost all trading brokerages offer intuitive trading charts that are interactive.

With a general overview of the fundamental market conditions, you should place a trade with the thought that you will be committed to the idea only as long as it takes to make a profit and close out the trade. Short-term time frames last from a few minutes to a few hours depending on the holding time of the trade. You can have several short-term perspectives as you buy, sell, and hold many different positions during your trading day. Each one of the trades is alive when it is open, and the risk will not go away until you close it out. If you keep short-term perspectives on each trade, you will be evaluating each trade on its own merit apart from the longer-term perspectives that helped you evaluate the market in the first place. If you use the long-term perspective to guide you but use the short-term perspective to evaluate each trade when you are in one, the combined effect will go a long way in keeping your day trading profitable.

Long-term perspectives usually involve time frames of three to six months and rely heavily upon fundamental analysis as well as technical chart evaluations.

This combination can lead to very convincing arguments as to overall market and trading conditions for a particular sector. For example, your broker might issue a report that trading in commodities will be profitable during the next six months but especially in the energy sector. You then evaluate the potential for each energy future, energy stock, and energy ETF trade with this overall perspective. It will also work out well if you included this sector in your daily review of market conditions in an effort to build up knowledge and familiarity of energy securities. You will then be able to use this sector knowledge, and a long-term perspective will help you evaluate potential trades with a short-term perspective.

Technical and Fundamental Analysis

Technical analysis refers to when the trader uses charts to predict the direction of the stock or trade. He looks at the chart of the past movement and overlays on the chart mathematically derived estimates of where the stock or trade will be in the future. He will then use this information to estimate where to place his trade. *Fundamental analysis* means using a company's financial documents, a country's growth rate, or other facts to predict the movement in a stock or trade.

A long-term perspective also includes macro knowledge of the overall world's economies and market conditions. These are the big-picture ideas: sovereign debt levels, currency strength, and the role of the world's developing economies are some of the subjects associated with a long-term perspective. These subjects take time to learn and don't often change that quickly. Again, country, market, and sector fundamentals are taken into account along with fifteen-minute, one-hour, and one-day technical charts (a one-day time frame chart might show the price movement history for the past two or three years).

WHAT SOFTWARE TELLS TRADERS

Your trading platform should provide you with the basic account information, access to news reports, and access to charts with different time frames. You might also see news reports coming across the newswire in one part of your screen and, of course, the price boxes of your watched securities—the flickering from green to red as the security moves up and down in price.

If you look at the activity section, you will see a history of your account including cash deposits, in and out trades, and daily interest payments (if your account has them). As you build up trades during the trading day, the open trades will show on the trades section where you can watch them go from the initial purchase into a profit zone as the market moves. If you have four, six, or more positions open, you can close them out one by one as they become profitable by opening up the close order box and waiting for the last possible moment to realize your gains. The gains will then be added to your balance, to your realized profit and loss, and to your buying power for the next round of trading. With your account software you can quickly look at your open positions and see what trades are in profit and which ones are in loss.

You can also use the charts to track an open position and get a graphic representation of your trade as it moves up and down. With this method you will be able to see your entry point marked on the chart. You can also draw a line on the chart to mark a point that will be your selling point. The graphic charts showing your trade as it creeps into a profit trade will give you a good idea of how the market is moving for that trading day.

Also, when you have built a hedged position, and your hedge has worked well, your trading software will tell you the overall net trade profit in percentages and dollar amount. When this happens you will be able to close out all of the components of the hedged trades with one click, allowing you to lock in the profits of the trade. Your software will then allow you to review the hedged trade for quality and effectiveness, as it is always important to see why a trade worked well and what can be improved.

THE BENEFITS OF PRACTICE ACCOUNTS

Using Play Money

You will do well if you have a brokerage account that allows the opening of a practice account or demo account for your use. These accounts have the same software and order-entry system as the live accounts. Your demo account will be off the books, will be funded with imaginary money, and all profits and losses will be on paper. These accounts can be very beneficial in giving you the opportunity to try out different leverage amounts, improve your order-entry skills, and allow you to try trading in different markets and sectors that you might not have experience with. You can also use the practice account to develop a disciplined investment technique and give yourself a chance to get used to trading and experiencing your reactions to the market's ups and downs without risking actual money.

When you use your demo account to place a trade that is according to your broker's recommendation, you can monitor it over time to evaluate the quality of your broker's advice. You can use a demo account to try out your own investment hunches, and use it to trade when it would otherwise be an inappropriate time to trade. For example, it might not be a good time to trade when the market is especially volatile, when there are uncertainties as to where the market is going, or when the risk levels associated with day trading are inappropriate to your personal situation.

Gains in a practice account will still make you feel very happy, especially when you win a big trade after interpreting the markets on your own, or when you plan out a hedge and it works in the way you intended. Overall, the use of practice accounts can go a long way in building day trading skills, gaining confidence, and keeping your account intact by giving you a way of trading during inappropriate market conditions.

Beware Short-Lived Demo Accounts

Make sure your brokerage firm offers a practice account that remains active during the whole time you have a live account open. Some brokerage firms offer demo accounts that are open for only a month and then automatically close. These practice accounts have to be reopened every month.

Before you begin to trade with real money, you will need to become comfortable with the order-entry system on your trading platform. You don't want to be worried about making a mistake in a trade—going long instead of short, putting in the wrong dollar amounts, wrong number of units, or wrong stop levels. Practice will also improve your finesse and confidence for closing out a trade when you need to, whether at a profit or a loss.

It is in your best interest to practice your trading platform's order entry and order closing many times while using your demo account. Start your order-placing training with scalping (trading using a five- to ten-minute time frame), and using small sums of money. Before each trade, write down the security or FX pairs and margin amounts you are going to use on paper before you place the order. This will give you time to think through the trade. You can make a decision about whether to go long or short as you see the market going. Don't worry about doing it very quickly at first, as speed will develop with practice.

AN EXAMPLE TRADE

For example, you could see that the overnight Asian and European markets have performed well. You could decide to go long (buy) 100 shares of a 3x S&P 500 ETF in an effort to capture the gains you think will be in the American markets. You would determine ahead of time that you would like to make a 5 percent profit out of the trade. After planning out the trade on paper, you would go into your demo account and set up the trade in the order-entry system of the trading platform. You would double-check your order, and then execute (place the trade).

Fight Against Stress

Emotions can run high during a typical day trading session. A lot of stress can be involved with trading large sums of money in an active and moving market. Use your demo account to get familiar with the high-pressure world of day trading without the risk of losing real money.

To learn the quick order-entry skills required for day trading, you should immediately open the close order box and monitor the profit/loss level until profit is shown in the trade. If the market is moving slowly or there is time until the 5 percent profit comes, take your profit early, before your profit goal is met. Your goal is to just get the feeling of making a round-trip trade.

MORE BEGINNER TIPS

Trading in and out in a few minutes with just a little bit of profit will go a long way in giving you skills and confidence. The key is to build on profitable trades to develop positive experiences going into and out of the market. Stick to one trade at a time, with round lots of one hundred shares, one thousand units of FX, etc., as it is best to develop skills one at a time. When you get used to round lots, you will think in terms of percentage profits with those trading numbers.

If the demo account offers a large sum to practice with (such as $100,000 or $250,000), don't overuse the account, as this will color your expectations as to dollar profit amounts. If you overuse the account and get used to placing big trades, you will get discouraged when you begin trading with an amount that is less than the amount in your demo account. It is best to trade a few rounds and take a break, since it is really easy to get tired when you are trying to learn this new skill. It is also human nature to get fatigued with making smaller trades for a long time and want to make one big trade for the day and quit. Resist this temptation, as this will not help you. Learning to trade is like learning a foreign language: it is better to have shorter learning sessions every day than to have one or two long sessions infrequently. It's very helpful to have a way to try out new strategies and ideas without trading in your live account. Keep a strategy notebook as a place to write down and plan your trading ideas. For example, keep track of:

- Day, time, month, season
- Overall market conditions
- Level of the US, European, and Asian market indexes
- Price of oil
- Price of gold
- The level of a commodity index
- The price of the major currency pairs

Use your notebook to write down your strategy and its source. For example, you could write, "Merrill Lynch advises to accumulate long exposure to NZD/USD at anything below 69." Note that today it is at 66, and the market has been down for the past three days. The Asian markets were up 1.5 percent overnight and now the European markets are up 0.5 percent. Thinking that you'll try out the theory that the US markets will follow when they open, you decide that a long NZD/USD position will be a good trade. After writing down all of the facts to the setup, you then place the trade in the demo account.

This trade will be separate from all other trades that you have going on in the demo account. Each trade is separate from the other because they were done for different "tests." With this trade, you must be extremely professional and cool-headed about the execution and strategy. For example, if the trade turns out wrong, you should let it ride until it corrects, checking it three or four times that day before finally closing it out at the end of the day, win or lose. When you monitor it, make marks as to the market conditions that led up to the trade, such as "the S&P went down for a fourth day," etc. Do not modify the trade, change stops, or add to the trade in any way.

What you are learning is how to spot setups using theory and how to build confidence by seeing a trade to the end. If there is an unannounced, unpredictable event such as a natural or manmade disaster or unannounced economic statement, then you should cancel out of the trade and void the experiment, as these things were not in the variables of the experiment. You can have several experiments going on in your demo accounts. They work best when you're emotionally vested in the success of the trade. If you plan, observe, and act in a cool, calm, and professional manner, you can learn a great deal. Keep track of the trade, and when the experiment is finished, take notes as to the time in its development, the market conditions that developed, and the profit that was made.

PAPER PROFITS, REAL EMOTIONS

Trading in your demo account will give you the greatest benefit when you feel the full emotions of winning and losing at day trading. When you are trading in your demo account, you experience the ups and downs of the markets, the thrill of the order entry, and the emotions related to profits and losses. It is important to feel the full emotions of success and failure, as this is one of the keys to learning how to be successful in day trading.

You will learn how to spot setups, how to manage your cash and margin amounts, and how to use a risk management program. When you are using the full educational benefits of a practice account, you will learn how to resist the temptation to close out of a losing trade because you are angry, when to take your profits without getting greedy, how to use moving stops (by using automatic trade closeouts to lock in profits), and when to take a loss.

Moving Stops

Moving stops are a way to continuously move the auto-sell function of the trading platform higher and higher, following the gains in the trade. If you do this, you will be riding your profits. If the stock goes up $5, you can adjust your auto-sell up $5 too, so you will not have to ride the trade back down to its original price if it turns into a losing trade before you sell it out. This way the trading software will automatically sell it at the higher price, ensuring you a bigger profit.

It is important to experience the full feelings of "ruling the markets" and "knowing everything" when you have a series of profitable trades, as well as experiencing taking on too much risk in search of more and more thrills. It's all right to have losing trades in your demo account. Every day trader should experience placing a big trade and losing in a big way. It is better to have paper losses and feelings of "I should have" with play money than to feel the pain in real dollars.

The more you can learn in the demo account, the better trader you'll be. Consider your demo account as lessons learned cheaply. You should take care of your demo account as you would a regular account: use care in the trades you are placing. Take a lot of ownership and pride in your demo account and build it up over time, just as you would a real account; it's a measure of your developing day trading skills.

Chapter 5

Handling Risk

Day trading would be very simple if it only consisted of buying and selling and making a profit. In the real world, there is the chance that a trade will go bad, that there will be a loss, or worse, many trades at one time could go bad and you'll wipe out your trading account. This is the risk associated with trading.

The best way to handle trading risk is to understand it, quantify it, and develop a method of using hedges and electronic programmed trading techniques to reduce the maximum percentage loss of your account. Risk is inherent to trading, but with a bit of math and the use of programmed trading methods, you can reduce it to an acceptable minimum.

RISK AND CASH ACCOUNTS

The Importance of Real Money

Before you begin trading you will need to have the right mind-set, thinking of your day trading account as a cash account. After you understand that this cash account can be used offensively and defensively and know how to strengthen it, the next step is the proper use of a margin account. Learning the mathematics of margin, its use, your account's buying power, and the possibilities of margin calls will complete your understanding of cash and margin management. We'll talk about margin a bit later; here let's concentrate on the importance of cash.

CAPITAL PRESERVATION AND YOUR CASH ACCOUNT

The primary objective of your trading account is capital preservation. With this in mind, you should think of your trading account as a cash account. This means that your account should be in cash all the time; you buy a security only when the situation presents itself and then return to cash. You should *prefer* to be in cash and not want to be in a trade, since being in cash minimizes risk. Risk, in this case, is the opportunity to lose money.

If your objective is to be in cash, then each trade can be viewed as a supplement to the normal interest rates that you would earn in the account. Depending upon the prevailing interest rates (which are quite low now), you will be earning interest on your cash balance—which is calculated at the overnight rate. In other words, the interest will be calculated to what you have in cash each night and will be more or less depending upon how much cash is in your balance and not in a trade. When you are in 100 percent cash, you are 100 percent safe, and you are earning interest. If you are earning an interest rate of 2.5 percent a year on a $50,000 balance, your interest accumulation would be $1,250 a year, or about $6.25 per trading day with no risk.

If you were accepting no risk or as little as possible, you would plan ways of adding to this daily accrual with as little an amount of risk as possible.

Hedge Fund Risk

Of course, not all investors think this way. In the world's largest hedge funds, all the cash they have in their accounts is invested in US government T-bills. In a separate account, they typically borrow against the T-bill deposit at a ratio of 4:1. This 4x leverage is amplified even higher when they day trade FX, futures, and commodities. If hedge fund managers were completely risk averse, they'd leave the money in T-bills, which are about as safe as you can get.

Granted, you have to take on a measured amount of risk while you are entering a trade, but if you approach the trading day with the thought that you will be adding to the $6.25 risk-free accrual, you will have the appropriate risk appetite for day trading. Remember, the cash in your account is what you will be using as a draw for your salary. In other words, your paycheck from the trading account will be in dollars, and you will be paying your bills associated with the operating of your day trading business in dollars; this is the balance that you should be looking to keep high. You don't want to load up your account in things other than dollars (stocks, FX, futures, etc.) for too long because you eventually have to convert these into dollars to spend.

TRADING AS A SOURCE OF INCOME

Remember, you are in the business of day trading to make money to pay for your expenses, buy the extras you want in life, and add to your overall net worth. When you think about always having to at some time convert the balance in your trading account back into money (dollars) that are usable for things other than securities—mortgage payments, car purchases, and living expenses, and so on—you will see your trading account as a source of income, a cash account on which you can draw at any time to pay for your expenses. When you think of it this way, chances are much less that you will run out of money (the dollars needed to pay your bills). If you do run out of money, after all, you will be forced to close shop. Proper cash account management can prevent this from happening.

OFFENSIVE AND DEFENSIVE RISK

Striking a Balance

In considering risk, you should think of your cash account in two terms: defensively and offensively. The defensive approach is to keep in mind that your cash account is the source of your paycheck and the source of a day trading business's self-sufficiency. The offensive approach focuses on getting into and exiting trades as a way of increasing your net worth.

THE DEFENSIVE RISK CASH ACCOUNT

While in the beginning as you build up your account you might take a lower paycheck as a draw from your account, you should think of your trading account as a cash account that has a balance big enough to get you to the next trading day. After all, that is your ultimate goal: to get to the next trading day. A defensive mind-set will pay the bills associated with trading out of the account with as small an amount of withdrawals as possible.

This means that not only will you be day trading part time while building up your account, but you might be able to switch to working part time before becoming a full-time day trader. All the while you should keep your cash withdrawals to a minimum by keeping your expenses associated with your day trading business low. If you have a full-service broker, they will most likely ask you, "What is this account's primary objective?" Even though your primary objective should be capital preservation, you should answer, "Capital appreciation." This will inform your broker what kind of advice you expect.

THE OFFENSIVE RISK CASH ACCOUNT

An offensive approach to risk regarding your cash account means focusing on entering and exiting trades with the thought of increasing your net worth, no matter how small the gain may be. You trade with the thought of building enough capital gains in your account on a daily, weekly, and monthly average so that you you'll have enough to pay for your expenses, draw a salary, and better your overall financial position. You use both short-term and long-term perspectives to aggressively search for enough trades throughout the week and month to meet your minimum gain requirement, plus an acceptable profit.

Trading Offensively and Defensively

It is best to think of your cash account in both defensive and offensive ways, often changing perspectives throughout the day as the trading conditions change. You might be offensive in the very early morning hours as you trade S&P 500 futures and switch to a completely defensive mode after your profit has been made or after a situation such as when the US markets open and become erratic in their movement. With time and experience, you will get very good at switching between these philosophies as the situation changes.

YOU DON'T ALWAYS HAVE TO TRADE

Remember, you don't always have to trade in every situation. In fact, if you have been playing your cash account the right way, both defensively and offensively, you can choose to sit out trading days when it is not clear you will make a profit. This way, your account will have enough profit and gains built into it to allow for a day off. Remember, you are looking for weekly and monthly *average* gains;

averaging gains will prevent you from forcing yourself to trade in every market condition.

STRENGTHENING YOUR CASH ACCOUNT

Most importantly, you must think of any loss that occurs in your day trading account as a withdrawal from the account—e.g., if you have a balance of $10,000 in your account and you make a monthly expense account withdrawal of $500 to pay for the expenses that are directly related to a month's day trading activity, and the same day you lose $500 in your account, you have then made a "withdrawal" from your day trading account of $1,000 for the day. To bring the account back up to the original buying power of the account, you will then have to make an additional $1,000 in profits to get the account back up to $10,000. This sounds simple, but when you think about strengthening your cash account, you should at the minimum think of always returning the balance to the original amount. In other words, you should be making money each month equal to the expenses associated with trading and replacing any losses you have incurred, plus an acceptable interest rate.

This is not as hard as it sounds, especially if you take a defensive approach to withdrawals by minimizing your expenses and only entering into trades that you have a very good chance of exiting with the same amount you entered with or better.

KEEPING YOUR CASH ACCOUNT INTACT

You should be always thinking of keeping your cash account intact. Keeping it intact means keeping it safe and ready for the next day's trading. You'd never want to get into the situation where your cash runs too much risk to the point where it might not last to the next trading day! With this in mind, you should enter into every trade with the idea that it will enhance your cash position. Your cash account doesn't just strengthen with increases; it strengthens with security and potential. For example, if you have a large enough balance in your account, you might be able to limit the size of the margin you are using on each trade to get into a trade that has a longer time frame to wait to make a profit on it. In other words, you can use more of your cash to make the trade, and less of your margin, and therefore reduce the overall risk of the trade. You won't have to squeeze every dollar out of your account: you can take less risk because the trades will take less of your margin.

If the fundamentals and the technical indicators are telling you that the trade is good, the opportunity to make money is very evident. There is still a risk involved, however, due to the holding length of the trade; the longer a trade, the greater the risk.

Total Return Strategy

The returns of your account are the combined interest accrual and trading gains; this is the true measure of your account's performance. This combined number is often called a total return strategy. Think of your trades in three groups: the safe trade, the risky trade, and the very risky trade. The safe trade is your cash balance and the short-term, small positions that you will close quickly. These trades will strengthen your cash account the most, but don't think that these small trades will generate enough profit to draw against. You are better off thinking about the profit generated from these small trades as adding to the buying power of your account through compounding; they also increase the margin available to you.

For every $10 you make in profit by trading one of these lower-risk trades, you will strengthen your cash account to the tune of $15–$5,000 worth of buying power, depending upon the margin amounts you are using (1.5:1 for equities and up to 500:1 for Forex).

CONTROLLING THE RISK OF EACH TRADE

Using Trading Plans

You can mitigate the risk of each trade with written trading plans. These can be as simple as entry points, expected time in the trade, and exit points. You can take the written plan one step further by setting a stop-loss order and a take-profit order at the time of the opening of the trade.

SETTING A STOP-LOSS ORDER

A stop-loss order is a way of automatically closing out of a trade. You precalculate the maximum loss you are willing to take in the trade and set this in the form of a stop-loss order. You thereby place a limit on the percentage and dollar amount of the potential loss of the trade. A take-profit order is the exact opposite: you enter beforehand the amount of profit in percentage or dollar amount that you would like to make on the trade. When the security meets the price level that is required to meet your preset profit amount, your trading platform will automatically close out the position and lock in your gains. Both stop-loss and take-profit orders are keys to planning a trade and are very good tools to use in effective active risk management of your day trading account.

The proper planning of a trading day always includes a review of the markets while scanning for potential day trading setups. After taking note of the setups that are available, you should then choose the best of these and go about the business of planning each trade before placing the orders.

Minimizing Risk

You wouldn't take a trip to a foreign country without telling someone where you were going and when you would be back. You can tell yourself where you are going with a trade and when you are coming back by setting profit and loss limits ahead of the trade. The next step is to use the stop-loss field of the order-entry screen to set the maximum amount of loss that can occur with this trade before the trade automatically closes out. You can program this loss amount to be small in relation to your overall account dollar size.

When you are ready to commit to a trade, call up the "place order" screen on your trading platform. The order screen will have fields for the symbol of the security, number of units, and the price at which it will execute. In addition to these fields, there are fields labeled "Take Profit" and "Stop Loss." As you enter in the number of units of the trade, the trade value in dollars will show as well as the margin used. Before you press the submit button and execute the trade, you can lock in your planned profit and limit the potential loss involved in this trade.

Using the "Take Profit" field, you enter the price of the security at which you would like to have the trading platform close the order automatically, locking in your gains.

RISK MANAGEMENT AND MOVING STOPS

With a proper risk management technique such as the 2 percent rule, the planned use of stop losses can prevent and control a major meltdown in a trade position. The 2 percent rule is defined as when each trade is preprogrammed through stop losses to close the order with no more than 2 percent of your total account balance lost. For example, suppose you have a $10,000 balance in your account, and you have an order on the books for one hundred shares of an energy ETF at $10 per share for a total of $1,000. You would place a stop-loss order at $8 ($10,000 × 2 percent = $200 maximum loss. $1,000 total position – $200 maximum loss = $800 minimum ending trade value. $800/100 shares = $8 per share). It takes a bit of working out on a calculator, but this method can be a very effective risk management tool. This is a good example of setting your expected profits before the trade is made. It's also a good example of day trading with a plan. You make this trade after consulting all relevant market indicators, news, and charts to get to the point where you are reasonably certain of a favorable outcome of the trade.

Automatic Moving Stops

There is often an option on your order-entry system on your trading platform to make a moving stop activate automatically: you can set the percentage, pip, or dollar amount that you would like to use. Your trading platform then automatically adjusts the moving stop up as the security moves up (or down, if you are shorting or selling the security).

Of course, there is the saying, "Cut your losses and let your profits run." In other words, you can move your stop losses up as the price of the security moves up. For example, if you place a trade for a stock at $15 and a stop-loss order at $12.50, you are $2.50 behind the market price of the stock. As the stock moves up in price, you would move the stop to exactly $2.50 behind the moving market price of the stock—i.e., if the stock moved to $18.75, you would move your stop to $16.25. This would trigger a closing-sell order at the new price of $16.25 and would lock in $1.25 in gains. As the stock moves higher from $18.75, you move the stop loss higher yet. This is referred to as a moving stop and can be a very effective tool in keeping your profits intact in moving markets.

Risk management methods such as the 2 percent rule and moving stops are a key element to keeping you in the game of day trading. Too many times day traders have built positions without regard to risk and lose considerable amounts of money when trades go bad.

In stock exchanges, stocks are bought and sold constantly. Large boards on the trading floor let traders know the last highest and lowest prices of a stock as well as other information needed to make profitable trades. Day traders examine stock performance as well as general market conditions before placing their trades.

Day trading (as well as other kinds of trading) is regulated by the Securities and Exchange Commission (SEC). Created in 1934 as part of President Roosevelt's New Deal legislation, the SEC's first chairman was Joseph P. Kennedy, father of future president John F. Kennedy. His staff included future Supreme Court justices William O. Douglas and Abe Fortas.

Stock markets exist in many countries around the world, such as the Royal Exchange in London, shown here. As a day trader this means you can trade virtually any time, day or night, because even when the market is closed in one country, other markets are open elsewhere around the globe.

Day traders often participate in what is called the foreign exchange market (Forex). Traders buy units of a foreign currency based on predictions about changes in the exchange rate with another foreign currency. When you go abroad and change your money for that of the country in which you're traveling, you are participating in a small way in the foreign exchange market.

Prior to 1971, the US dollar was directly convertible into gold at a fixed price. In an attempt to combat the ongoing monetary crises, President Richard Nixon took the US off the gold standard. The result was that the price of gold fluctuated and has continued to do so ever since, offering many opportunities to day traders to make money.

Photo Credit: © Global Cuts

A futures contract is an agreement to purchase something in the future. If you take a long position on wheat futures, you're predicting that the price of wheat will rise so that the value of the contract you have purchased will be greater than it is now. If that happens, you'll be able to sell the wheat futures contract at a higher price than the amount you paid for it.

Successful day traders must track world economic and political developments, watching for changes that may affect their trades. The price of oil, for example, can be affected by such things as the weather, the season, political tensions, and the growth of alternate energy sources.

One phenomenon that can negatively affect day traders is a bubble. This occurs when the price of something is artificially inflated and eventually collapses. In 2008, the US housing bubble burst, and artificially inflated home prices collapsed. Millions of families lost their homes to foreclosure, and property values plunged.

The Dow Jones Industrial Average is a stock market index made up of thirty companies. The Nasdaq is an American stock exchange. Both are important market indicators which day traders follow closely, attempting to gauge the overall health of the market.

Day trading can be a full- or part-time job, depending on your temperament and how much money you want to make from it. You need a high-speed Internet connection. You also need reliable sources of market information such as *The Wall Street Journal* or CNBC, advice from your brokerage, and annual reports and financial statements from companies whose stock you're trading.

A Japanese candlestick chart shows the movement of a stock by depicting the high price and low price of the security, as well as its opening and closing price, during a given period (usually a day). Day traders use candlestick charts to perform technical analysis of a stock, studying its movements and identifying patterns that signal buy or sell opportunities.

Chapter 6

Trade Setups and Information

Knowing what you'd like to trade and what market is the first step. The next step is scouring the markets looking for good and profitable trades. For each trade that is a quick, easy profit, there are ten or more that are potential losers. Knowing what to look for in a trade is the key: these are your trade setups, and you'll find them by looking at market information.

HOW DOES MARGIN WORK?

Your Cash Account's Buying Power

Buying on margin is like buying securities with a credit card. You can buy more than you have with only the cash in your account. This leads to bigger trades and potentially bigger profits. When you have your day trading account set up with the ability to use margin, you have to the ability to put up cash and securities as collateral in a loan to buy more securities.

Margin is much like making a down payment on a purchase of something tangible, such as a car or a house. With both of them, you put down a required amount and finance the rest. With a car it is often 10 percent down and financing is 90 percent; with a house you put down 20 percent and finance 80 percent. When you are financing stock, futures, or FX with margin, you are putting down anywhere from 2 percent to 66 percent of the total amount of securities purchased.

For example, using margin you would need to put down $660 for each $1,000 worth of stock or ETFs purchased, and $20 for each $1,000 worth of FX purchased at a 50:1 margin in a Forex account. This loan between you and your brokerage house is opened and closed with each round trip of securities trading. In this way, your available margin goes up and down depending upon the number and size of trades you have open during the day. The brokerage will constantly adjust the amount available as you open and close trades.

You might wonder what margin level you should use when you're trading. When starting out it can be easier to use a lower margin ratio with your trades, since it lowers the impact of a fast market. You could, however, set your margin level at the point that you would use it normally and train yourself from the start to place trades with higher leverage.

The margin available in your account will move up and down, as the trades that are open move up and down in profit and loss dollar amounts. The amount of margin available to you for trading is directly tied to the size of your account. Cash plus the available margin equals the buying power of your account. That buying power is added to and subtracted from with the gain and loss of each trade. Because day trading is dynamic, if your trades are highly leveraged, the margin and buying power in your account can move quite rapidly.

THE MATHEMATICS OF MARGIN

Since margin acts as a multiplier on the upward and downward movement of each security, it is really important to understand the mathematics of how it works. First, set the amount of margin you would like to use. If you would like to use 50 percent margin on a hundred-share purchase of a stock ETF, you need to pay for it with two-thirds down and the other one-third with margin. If the initial purchase is $15,000, you need to have $10,000 cash and $5,000 margin available.

Let's say that the market is having a really good day. The ETF that you bought is up 10 percent for a gain of $1,500. Your actual percentage gain is much higher than 10 percent. It is calculated by dividing the dollar gain by the actual amount invested: $1,500 divided by $10,000, resulting in a 15 percent profit on actual capital invested.

This is an illustration of the multiplier effect of the margin on profits. Adjust the level of margin you use in a trade to fit the amount of risk associated with that security. For example, you know that the

S&P 500 has lower volatility than an individual stock, ETF, leveraged ETF, FX pair, or commodity (this is due to the fact that the S&P 500 is comprised of five hundred of the largest stocks in the US markets, and therefore is internally diversified, as opposed to trading only one stock); use higher amounts of leverage for these positions. Other sectors, such as the financial sector, are very volatile; use lower amounts of margin to reduce risk.

The same dramatic amplification can be shown on losses, since the mathematics of margin works to the downside as well. In the same example, you put up $10,000 in cash and use $5,000 in margin to buy $15,000 worth of the stock ETF. The market is having a rough day, and the sector you are trading goes to the downside of 10 percent. Because you're trading on margin, your losses are amplified much like when there were gains. To calculate the losses, divide the loss amount by the total actual capital investment: $1,500 divided by $10,000, or a loss of 15 percent. Margin acts as a lever to increase the percentage movement in the stock, ETF, currency, or future.

MARGIN LIMITS

The maximum amount of margin that you are able to use in your brokerage account is limited by the type of security you are day trading. Market regulators are the ones who are in control of what amount of margin can be used in stock, ETF, and futures accounts. This is because some of the world's worst economic problems have been brought about by overspeculation in the financial markets. Overspeculation often causes a bubble in the market. This allows greater and greater price expansion in the market until eventually the bubble bursts and the market plunges. Overheated markets and market bubbles have occurred many times throughout history.

Market regulators attempt to control the formation of bubbles by regulating the amount of leverage allowed in trading securities. On the low side, regulators allow 5:1 margin. The high side of the amount of margin allowed is the unregulated Forex markets, in which the amount of margin allowable in an account can range from 10:1 to 500:1.

MARGIN CALLS

Margin call refers to a situation in which the broker or stock exchange determines that the market value of the stocks being used as collateral for margin has fallen below what the broker or exchange perceives as their value. If this happens, the broker or exchange issues a "call" and traders are required to add additional cash to the account or provide more collateral. If they can't do it, the broker has the right to sell the stocks that are being used as collateral.

For example, suppose you have highly leveraged the purchase of an FX pair, have used much of your available margin to buy it, and losses put you in a position where you are below the minimum equity in the trade. When this happens, your broker will issue a margin call. Now you must put up more capital (usually cash) in order to get the equity in your position high enough to meet the minimum. Some brokers allow you until the end of the trading day to fund the account, while others begin to systematically sell off parts of your portfolio in order to meet the margin. Others immediately close out the position when it meets a level that is below the minimum.

A margin call can be disastrous to your trading account. They usually happen when the market is at its worst, and the value of your stock, future, or FX pair has dropped well below what you intended it to be. When this happens, you can be forced to sell at a loss, without the time to be in the trade until your security recovers in value. Calls can be especially costly when a position is closed out without notice, as this takes out all capital involved in the trade.

Often a margin call comes when you are not monitoring your positions, such as when you are away from your computer, during an overnight trade, or during an otherwise unwatched longer time frame trade. If you are making highly leveraged trades, keep an extra cushion of available margin in your account. In any case, a margin call can be disruptive to your trading, either by requiring you to deposit more capital or by the positions closing.

You can guard against margin calls through cautious use of high margin ratios and active position size management, such as the pyramid method. Pyramiding is a method of building trading positions in three separate groups and closing out the positions one at a time. This is done to average in your cost and selling prices to lock in gains and prevent a large position being established at an unfavorable price. This way you are getting the average of the price of the trade over time, and if the trade moves up or down, you'll get the average of the prices over the length of the trade, further eliminating the risk that you bought and sold at a less than ideal price.

As discussed earlier, other methods to prevent margin calls include the 2 percent rule and stop-loss settings (automatic closing of a position) to limit the overall loss of a position to 2 percent of the cash balance of your total day trading account. This 2 percent limit would, in theory, allow you to have fifty consecutive losing trades before your account had a balance of zero (50 × 2 percent = 100 percent).

LEARN TO TRADE OPPORTUNISTICALLY

Profitable Trades in Any Market

You can develop your day trading skills to the point that you have a feel for the market and have the ability to make a plan that will get you to your objectives. Day trading objectives can be set each session, but you should make them for every position with the use of a profit and loss limit for every trade. If you can incorporate some basic risk management techniques and moving stops, you are a long way toward being ready for your first trade.

GET A FEEL FOR THE MARKET

The thought of your first real money trade can be both frightening and exciting. In order to ensure a successful and enjoyable experience, it is best to make sure you are ready. This readiness comes from having a firm grip on where the market is, where it's going, and how you can ride its movement to capture gains. An honest assessment of your financial market awareness can go a long way in knowing if you are ready to place that first trade. It also serves as a yardstick to measure your confidence and assurance of the profit of that trade.

You should develop a few favorite sectors that you monitor on a daily basis. They might be your favorite vacation spot's currency paired with your home country's currency. It might be the price of oil or some other commodity that you use on a daily basis. It might be an index of the market itself, either a measure of the S&P 500, the Dow 30, or the Nasdaq.

GET SET UP IN A DEMO ACCOUNT

A really good way to develop a base point of reference for a market's index or individual security is by using your demo account. You can place one trade in your demo account for each of the indexes, sectors, and securities you trade and use the notes section of your trading platform to mark them as baseline market levels. Because markets and prices are always moving, you can begin to look at the price levels of a sector at any point of your development. This is your starting point, your baseline to which you make all comparisons.

When in the process of establishing a baseline for the market, it is best to give yourself time to see a change in the underlying price of the sector. If you don't do this, you may assume that market is always and has always been at that level.

Much like the fashion world, what seems in vogue during one season often turns out to be unfashionable by the next season or fashion cycle. It is best to keep this analogy in mind when evaluating the price levels of a commodity, future, FX pair, index, or ETF. If you watch a sector long enough you will see it change in price, fall out of favor, or otherwise shift in sentiment. Securities prices are always changing. When you hold off from establishing a position until you witness this change, you will have a sense of the historical performance of that sector. It really helps you decide to establish a position in a security when you know that last month, season, or year that same security was 10 percent higher, 10 percent lower, or worse.

Long-term observations of the market will help you understand what sectors have been worth and how prices can change over time, whether quickly or slowly. Markets move in patterns, as shown in technical analysis, and trading setups can be repeating in pattern. If you do not allow enough time to develop a feel for the market, you will be trading blind, with only your charts and fundamental analysis to guide you. While these are very good tools, a knowledge of where the target stock, ETF, future, or commodity has been will give you a greater sense of where they can go, whether they're likely to increase or decrease in value.

MAKING A PLAN

Before you place your first trade, it is best to plan the trade from beginning to end. When you are starting to trade, it is often very easy to get caught up in the moving markets and forget your original objective. If you have a written plan for each trade, you will have a record of the entry point, expected length of the trade, expected exit point of the trade, and expected outcome of the trade. Writing down the goals of a trade will give you control of your daily, weekly, and monthly overall day trading profit. It will also teach you to enter into each trade with a clearly defined outcome. You should know before you open a trade at what point you expect to close it and lock in your profits.

This thinking through the trade before committing to it will help you keep control over your trading. If this is not done, you will get into the habit of opening and closing trades at any point of the market, with no goal other than to make money.

A Trading Goal of "Making Money"

To say that your trading goal is making money is not a plan. You should treat your day trading like a business, and the capital in your account should be treated as an asset to reach your goals. In order to reach your goal of having a profitable day, week, or month day trading, each trade must be planned. It is better to have three or four well-planned trades during the day than to engage in a series of rapid-fire opening and closing of trades without any thoughts to their placement.

Many sports coaches teach their players to visualize personal goals during training sessions. A weightlifting coach might tell the trainees to visualize themselves lifting certain target amounts. A gymnastics coach might tell the team members to visualize making a perfect landing after a vault. Visualization is often a key to many top athletes reaching their goals. Remember, you are building the balance of your cash account in order to have a surplus, hopefully enough to make a withdrawal from the account at the end of the month to pay your expenses and give yourself a salary. Successful businesspeople evaluate potential investments carefully and rank each one on its own merit and potential. Even though they may have the means to get financially involved with every deal that comes across their desk, they are wise enough to limit what they get into. They have learned to be patient and wait for only the best deals.

When a trade is profitable, you can get out of it and generate additional cash for your account. When a trade turns unfavorable, you are stuck with it. When it closes out at a loss, you are weakening your account and day trading business.

Get Some Exercise!

Trading during volatile times can lead to stress. It is good to use exercise to help you get through emotionally upsetting markets. Going to the gym, playing outdoor sports, mall walking, and even cleaning out the garage can help you relieve stress, as the physical activity can help you refocus yourself toward positive day trading.

TRADING IN AN OVERHEATED MARKET

Riding Wild Market Swings

Most times the market operates in a well-organized manner with predictable unidirectional sector moves. Other times the market can be emotional and behave erratically. These times of extreme upward and downward movements can be an excellent opportunity to keep a cool head and make money by getting into trades at the bottom or top of valleys and peaks.

Market emotions come in two forms: euphoria and panic. In the euphoric stage, most market participants share the same good feelings: the market is going to go up, up, up! However, euphoria in the markets can come and go very quickly. All it takes is one bad piece of information to end the good feelings of traders and they will take their profits, or worse yet, begin shorting their positions. Your goal is to spot these euphoric feelings at their peak and short the sector they are in, or even short the whole market with a bear ETF, shorting an ETF, or even shorting an S&P 500 future. Often taking a position that makes money when the market goes down can be a safe bet, especially when all seems too rosy to be true.

READING THE SIGNS

The key is knowing when the market has reached its top and when it's the best time to include short trades in your portfolio. This is hard to gauge: in fact, no one will really know for sure. One of the best signs is when it seems that everyone is talking about the market:

how good it is, how much money they are making, how this guy they know made a killing in this stock or that and now is driving a Ferrari, etc. This is a good sign, because the general public usually gets into the market at the mid to late end of the market cycle, when the market has been going though a good period for long enough to seem an easy, safe bet again. What to do? The answer is simple: if the market seems to be getting overheated, place a few hedges in your account; keep a tight reign on your stops (don't let a trade go without one!); and use proper hedging techniques. This may mean diversification as well as the use of a bear ETF.

On the other hand, panic can also take over markets, causing very steep declines in short periods. These are usually brought on by sudden reports of bad news such as a natural disaster or political problems. The bad mood may flow from the mood of the general public as well. These are good times to begin building long positions in the affected market. If you are going to build positions either to the long or to the short of the market or sectors during these times, it is good to keep in mind that while it is likely the market will change direction, it is often impossible to determine when the change will actually take place.

To counteract this uncertainty, take smaller than usual bites of the sector and use the pyramid method, but with your accumulation spread out over longer time frames, such as a week to ten days. The goal is to set up a longer time frame trade, much like an FX carry trade that takes up to a month to go from start to finish. You enter into and exit each trade each day but continue to build on those positions during the month: the stock of ETF might be "in play" during a longer time frame, allowing you to capture the gains daily, but at a new price level each day as it gains in value over time. With this in mind, you need to think of the new price of the ETF or stock as it moves along in time, and not at the same price it was at the previous trading sessions. In other words, if XYZ was at $75 at the beginning of the week and you were trading it, and it was in play over a longer term, it might be at $85 at the start of the next week (and therefore $82 might be considered a good entry or buy price, whereas the week before, $82 would be considered an exit or sell price at a good profit).

If you are building a position on the extreme dips (long positions) or peaks (short positions), the total return of the positions can be impressive when the market corrects itself. The key is to build the trade so if it goes against you for a while it will not be detrimental to your account; use stops, and limit total margin to prevent extreme downward swings in value.

Building a Position in a Panicked Market

In a panicked market, it is best to break down your position building as in the pyramid method described earlier, but instead of using three entry points, you use around four to six spread out evenly over the length of the market's panicked mood. Use the standard three-point exit strategy to close out the position. This is a diverisfication of trade position built up of six entry points instead of the usual three in the typical pyramid method.

How can you tell it is a good time to build a position in the market during these times of highs and lows? You will know when the news of the market flows into the daily conversation of the general public. The market and its sectors are usually only discussed by the general public when they are at extremes. When all is rosy and it seems that there is "free money" to be made trading in the stocks, FX, and commodities, everyone will be talking. You'll hear conversations in line at the grocer, at the bookstore, and at the dentist's office. When things are going really good, Main Street gets involved, for better or for worse. If the market is really bad, these same people will talk about how the market will never come back, etc. The key phrase to listen for is, "things are different now." This is a sure sign that the market is either at a peak or a valley, people are feeling either very good or very bad, and that it is a good time to go in the opposite direction in the market. Much like doing the opposite of what you feel, if you do the opposite of what the market feels, you can have impressive returns in your account.

TRADING IN THE WORLD MARKETS

Using an Offshore Account

You can invest in foreign stocks, foreign indexes, and the indexes of developing parts of the world. This global investing can be done with an ETF in a US-based brokerage firm. For a truly global experience, though, you can open an account at one of the international firms known as offshore brokers. These accounts are easy to set up but are in some ways a bit more difficult to get money into and out of.

If you open up an offshore account at one of the many investment houses available, you would have to fill out a special tax form and file it with the IRS, indicating that you are the owner of an account that is held outside of the United States and its territories. Not to worry, though, as the form is easy to fill out and can easily be handled by a CPA or tax attorney.

Popular jurisdictions for offshore accounts include Luxembourg, Switzerland, Austria, Cyprus, and the Isle of Man. These accounts offer you access to the markets and investment products that are unavailable through a US-based account.

Don't be put off by the thought of opening up an offshore account. Contrary to recent news, they are not illegal. What is illegal is when a US-based holder of an offshore account does not report to the IRS the fact that the offshore account is held by the tax filer.

TRADING THE WORLD FX MARKETS

Some foreign exchange traders use the trading platform provided by their brokers to program buy and sell orders in the evening in order to trade with the European and Asian market time zones. The Asian stock market and economic news usually comes out from seven p.m. to one a.m. Eastern time, and the European news overlaps at one a.m. to six a.m. Eastern time. If a trader wants to get into the trades of the Asian and European currencies, he'll be trading with those economic area news reports, which then means trading at that time of the day.

Using their market knowledge of entry and exit points, day traders predetermine their profits for each trade. You can set trades the night before, and before you go to work in the morning, check your accounts to find the orders executed, locking your profits while you slept. It is important to keep track of the dates when important economic announcements will be made. You can go to the websites of the reserve banks of the world's major countries and economies to get an overview of when announcements will be made and when economic reports will be released.

Chapter 7

Analyzing the Market

Looking for trade setups is best done in a scientific manner. Tried and true techniques of looking for the best time to buy and sell securities lies in two forms: fundamental analysis and technical analysis. Fundamental analysis looks at the internal accounting of a company or the economies of a country, whereas technical analysis looks at the charts of a security and uses past trends to predict its future path.

FUNDAMENTAL ANALYSIS

Evaluating the Market

Reading the fundamentals is the process of knowing the economic or financial statements of a country, market, sector, or security. A company's financial statements can tell you how well the company is doing; you'll need to look for information on a company's structure, earnings per share (EPS), and P/E to give you these clues. You'll also have to analyze the supply and demand of commodities and the fundamentals of the world's economies and currencies. Last, you should know the shortfalls of using fundamentals as a tool to predict a security's future price.

KNOWING THE COMPANY OR SECTOR

When you are first learning how to read the fundamentals, it is important to find and read as many sources of information about the country, market, sector, or security as possible. This is how you really get to know the product you are going to day trade. You can find out about the fundamentals of a country by performing an Internet search for the central bank and/or national bank of that country. Links to the world's central banks can also be found on the Bank for International Settlements' website: www.bis.org. Read through the documents and cross-reference them with the information provided by your broker. Some brokers provide a semiannual report on different regions of the world economy. These are also excellent places to find a bird's-eye view of the economy and investing (trading) outlook of some of the world's countries.

If you are thinking about or are currently day trading a company or sector, you can sign up to receive Rich Site Summary (RSS) feeds about the security as news is reported. Some independent news services also offer this service. Signing up can be as simple as filling out a form and providing your email address. Your broker can also be a source for a market overview and can often produce a monthly sector guide as well. Full-service firms do especially well at this, but some of the independent discount brokers use the piggy-back method of offering the research of a full-service firm they are in association with.

Individual firms' literature, 10-Ks, past annual reports, and press releases can be found on company websites and are good sources when looking for specific information, such as a company's cash flows, balance sheet, etc. Individual companies' and sectors' research reports written by your broker, online conference calls sponsored by companies, and online conference calls sponsored by the different departments of your brokerage firms (FX, equities, commodities, etc.) are also excellent sources of the information for performing a fundamental analysis of a security.

LOOKING AT FINANCIAL STATEMENTS

When looking at financial statements, begin with the annual report. Here you will find the letter to stockholders, which tells them how the company has been doing and where it would like to go in the future. The letter to shareholders also explains the nature of the business operation. The income statement shows sales, expenses, and net income; this is shown over a twelve-month period. The balance sheet shows cash, what is owed to the company (accounts receivable), and fixed assets. These include equipment, buildings, land, and vehicles. The balance sheet also shows the value of any intellectual property such as patents and trademarks. Finally, the balance sheet shows any intangible assets, such as the value of goodwill. Goodwill is the value that the business puts on the synergy of the business—the synergy of the business is how their customers are better served by the company operating as a whole unit, as well as the value of their repeat customers. The balance sheet also shows liabilities, both short-term and long-term debts of the company.

Truth in Reporting

How do you know that a company is being truthful in their financials? All public companies are required by regulation to have their books audited by a licensed CPA firm. Companies usually take great pride when an auditor gives them his stamp of approval on a set of financial documents. There are exceptions to the rule, of course, such as the financial misconduct of Enron that came to light in 2001–2002.

The last thing a balance sheet shows is the stockholders' equity. This equity is a representation of the difference between what the company owns and what it owes.

You should also examine the statement of cash flows for the company. This shows how money flowed in, out, and through the company during the same year as the income statement. The statement of cash flows shows how the company sourced the cash needed for its internal growth: it shows whether the cash was internally generated through sales during the normal course of business, through the sale of an asset, or through the raising of cash through the sale of debt or equity stakes in the business.

STRUCTURE

Capitalization refers to the market value of a company. In the simplest terms, it is the share price multiplied by the number of outstanding shares minus the company's long-term debt. This is often called the structure of the company, and the amount of debt in relation to the amount of equity in the company will tell you how conservatively the company is structured; the lower the amount of debt, the more conservative. This is because during a slow economy (when sales might be off and the company does not produce as much cash), there is, in proportion, less debt to service. Therefore the company can make fewer payments toward its debt and use more to pay for other things to keep the company running. The capital structure of a company is usually carefully planned. In fact, there is thought to be a perfect balance between debt and equity on a company's balance sheet. The formula used to find this optimal mix is called the weighted average cost of capital, or WACC.

Trading During Earnings Seasons

During some times of the year it can be especially difficult to day trade. For example, stocks report their earnings quarterly, during what is often called earnings season. These generally fall during January, April, July, and October. During earnings season, companies can exceed or miss what the market expected their profits to be, and this can lead to exaggerated and unpredictable movements in a stock's price.

The WACC varies depending upon the cost of debt and the tax bracket of the corporation. This also means that if they keep the level of debt down, they will have a greater chance of being able to service the debt they already have. This will mean the company can maintain a high credit rating; when a company keeps a high credit rating it can get lower rates on its debt in the future. This leads to even lower debt service payment, making the company even healthier.

Cash flow will tell you if the company is financing their growth from their own generated sales, from the sale of assets, or from raising money externally. Of course, the best way a company can raise money is from its own operations, which are the company's normal course of business. This is shown in the "cash flows from operations" section of the cash flow statement.

The other sections tell you if the cash for the company is generated from the sale of assets, under the cash flows from investing. In other words, the financial section called the cash flow statement will tell you if the company is raising cash though its normal operations (for example, Apple earns cash through sales of its iPads, computers, and iPhones) or from the sale of an asset (for instance, if Apple sold off an office building somewhere). Clearly, cash raised during normal operations is the best, because the trader can assume that the company is in that type of business and that those normal operations (whether manufacturing, wholesale, retail, or service) will continue into the future. If cash goes up quarter after quarter, year after year, then that is the sign of a company that is in good health.

If the company is selling off assets to raise cash or produce a profit, this is a bad sign, because what happens when the company does not have any more assets to sell? A company should be providing the majority of their cash flows from operations if they want to have a sustainable business.

EPS AND P/E RATIOS

Earnings per share, or EPS, is found by taking the net earnings and dividing it by the total number of shares outstanding. If a company had $10 million in earnings and the number of shares is one million, the EPS would be 10. EPS of companies can range from 1:6, meaning $1/6 shares outstanding, up to 1:250, 1:500, or higher. If the company is just starting out and doesn't have much earnings, the EPS can be astronomical, in the hundreds, as the company is basically not earning. Believe it or not, these low profitable stocks can sometimes be the "darlings of the market" because these companies often are at the cutting edge of technology, and their product (while not as profitable as that of a traditional or established company) may be perceived as the wave of the future, with high demand expected soon. Startups are often in this category, as are high-tech companies. These stocks can be the high-flyers of the market, with gains of 5–10 percent daily, and—to sound a cautionary note—corrections of 10–20 percent daily are quite common as well. Risky? You bet, but it's the percentage movement up and down that makes traders love these stocks. Car payments, mortgages, kid's private tuition can be paid by trading these stocks day in and day out. If the company actually makes it to profit, well, who cares? By that time a new "darling of the market" will be around, capturing the hearts of traders worldwide.

Another method of looking at the price of a stock or ETF is the P/E ratio, which is the price of the stock divided by its earnings. P/E ratios can tell you how expensive a stock or ETF is compared to others in the investment universe. The lower the number, the cheaper the stock. If a stock has a higher than usual P/E numbers, this might be an indicator that the stock has crept up in value in relation to others in its industry sector. It may also indicate that it is a good time to short the stock because, all things being equal, companies in the same industrial sector usually have close to the same P/E ratio. When one is out of whack from the others, this usually means that that stock or ETF is undervalued or overvalued compared to the others in its class.

MEASURING SALES GROWTH

Another method of determining if a company is doing well is measuring its sales growth. The sales growth of a company can be found by looking at the sales of the previous three to five years. There should be clear indications as to a growing sales base: there should definitely not be shrinking sales numbers. This would indicate that something is wrong with the product or management of the company.

FUNDAMENTALS OF COMMODITIES AND CURRENCIES

The Underlying Numbers

Commodities gains and losses are unrelated to the stock market. Grains, gold, oil, and copper often move higher when the equities market is stagnant. This means you can look for profitable trades even when the stock market is seemingly going nowhere and profitable trades are far and few between.

COMMODITIES GROWTH

From the mid-1960s to the early 1980s stock markets all over the world did not increase in value, but commodities did very well during these times. Unlike equities and equity futures, commodities have a limited supply. The supply is in a glut when the world's economies are doing poorly, and the supply is tight when the world's economies are doing well. Developing countries, such as China and India, use enormous amounts of raw materials in their ever-growing industrial sectors. China has the most demand; they have demand for soft commodities, grains, and industrial metals.

China and India also have a large appetite for gold, as this is often a preferred store of wealth for the people who live in these countries. While the supplies of commodities are limited and inelastic, the world's supply of money is ever changing. Money supply moves up and down according to the actions of the central banks and treasuries of nations across the world. The money supply of the world's currencies is increasing and decreasing in waves, and in long drawn-out time frames. For instance, during the 2008 economic crisis, many of the world's central banks expanded their money supplies to huge levels; in some cases, record amounts of money were added to the supply.

What does this mean for gold? Well, the best way to think of gold is that it, too, is a form of money. You can't buy a coffee or pay your rent with it, yet the Federal Reserve has euros, yen, other currencies, and gold in its reserves. Why? Because gold is a currency! So, if gold is inelastic and has a limited supply, and USD and other currencies are expanding rapidly, there is more USD, EUR, JPY, etc. in people's pockets to buy a relatively stagnant quantity of gold available for sale. What does this cause? Lots of money chasing few goods, and people with more money (through the money supply going up) being able to pay more and more for the fixed-supply asset (gold, or other property, such as real estate). The consequence is that the price will rise. More and more dollars chasing a fixed supply of goods equals an inflated price of the good.

LOW INTEREST RATES EQUAL HIGHER COMMODITIES PRICES

When there are excessively low interest rates in a country, this usually signals a large supply of money. This is because central bankers lower interest rates for only one purpose: to make loans cheaper for borrowers. The central banks want people to borrow, borrow, borrow, and spend, spend, spend. If a country's economy is slow, the central bankers will keep lowering interest rates until it gets so cheap to borrow money that everyone is borrowing. People will borrow to buy cars, clothes, houses, washers and dryers, as well as commercial loans such as borrowing for machines to produce goods and loans to buy inventory to sell. All the borrowing means more and more goods need to be produced to meet demand, which then means more and more jobs are created to produce the goods that are being bought. Those people who work at Macy's, Barneys New York, and Home Depot will then be working extra hours (because of all the people buying)—and they will have bigger payroll checks and be able to spend that extra money too, or use it to make payments on yet more loans. It's a domino effect, and it works quite well.

If you'd like to trade commodities, it's best to know a bit about them and where their demand comes from, since not all commodities act the same at all times. Some are in play during peak months or during peak times of the world economy, only to fall off and be stuck in the mud during slow economic times (which may last years!).

Oil is in limited supply, and it is difficult to discover new sources of this commodity. Oil is used by almost the whole world, as nations rely on oil in the progress of their economies. Natural gas is used to heat homes and process products throughout the world; it is difficult to source natural gas, and difficult to get it to its end user. Metals are in high demand and include copper, silver, iron, as well as other industrial metals. In fact, demand is so high for some metals that there is a significant scrap industry, such as the iron and steel scrap industries that make shipments to China. The grains and soft commodities include corn, sugar, and others; these are renewable, but demand increases when the world's economies are growing quickly.

COMMODITIES TRADING IN THE PAST AND PRESENT

In the 1980s and 1990s there was a slowing in the demand for commodities, and this led to a bear market and lessening of prices overall. Commodities are now considered inexpensive, and the 1980s and 1990s bear market caused a lessening in the production capacities of those producing commodities. This could cause a steep supply/demand ratio as the world's economies start expanding at full force.

The ever-expanding money supply will create a supply-and-demand imbalance, as there will be more dollars, yen, and euros chasing the same or fewer amounts of commodities. This will lead to a steady upward pressure in the price of commodities.

Since most commodities are now traded electronically in the futures markets, there are very few barriers to entry, and professional money managers, commodity hedgers for companies (professional financial firms that hedge commodities for their clients, such as a small airline, a trucking company, a family office based in Houston that has too much of its assets invested into oil and oil-related investments, etc.), and speculators can get into the business of commodity trading worldwide with just an Internet connection. The commodities market is a worldwide market and knows no borders. It can potentially be a very good place to set up shop and can lead to profitable day trading sessions for those who are willing to master the fundamentals of this area of trading.

CURRENCY FUNDAMENTALS

In general, most currencies are allowed to float up and down against the values of other currencies as dictated by market forces. In some cases, the governments or central banks will attempt to regulate the value of their currencies through the practice of intervening in the markets. This is done by the government or central bank buying or selling its own currency in the interbank market in an attempt to force a change in value of that currency.

If the central bank would like to increase the value of the country's currency, it sells off its foreign currency reserves and uses the proceeds to buy its home currency. This action pushes up the price of the home currency while pushing down the price of the foreign currency. If the country would like to make its currency go down in value, the central bank increases its amount of foreign currency reserves by buying currency in the open market with its home currency. This increases the amount of the home currency in relation to the foreign currency; the effect is to lower the price of the currency. This is referred to as quantitative easing and was done heavily by the Swiss National Bank after the 2008–2009 worldwide banking crisis. This event, and others related to it, caused the Swiss franc, commonly known as the Swissy or CHF, to rapidly and dramatically rise in value against other currencies, including the euro and the US dollar. Since the Swissy gained so much against Switzerland's trading partners, Swiss exports were stunted, and the Swiss economy began to slow. The Swiss had effectively established a "peg" to the euro, with the result being the Swiss franc moved up and down in tandem with the movement of the euro. This was done by very actively entering into the market with huge daily trades timed and placed to keep the Swissy at a fixed exchange rate with the euro. It was very difficult and needed constant adjusting (as the euro would fluctuate daily) but it was thought to be the best because the European Union (home of the euro) was Switzerland's main trading partner.

While this made the Swiss franc a stable, reliable, and low-interest currency, the Swiss National Bank dramatically "lifted the peg" of the Swiss franc/euro on January 15, 2015. The Swiss central bankers did so without warning, causing the Swiss franc to jump in price against the world's currencies. Currency traders and currency brokers alike were bankrupt overnight, as they couldn't protect their accounts from such immediate and drastic price movements. Many trading houses and hedge funds viewed the event as a disaster.

A similar situation could happen in China, where the price of the Chinese yuan is pegged to the US dollar at a rate that might not be sustained in relation to all of the exporting that China is doing with the United States. The yuan is now beginning to be revalued and is appreciating against the US dollar.

BRETTON WOODS AND THE GOLD STANDARD

Under the Bretton Woods system, the US dollar was linked to gold. The Bretton Woods system was an agreement that was set up after World War II in an effort to help the war-ravaged countries of Europe re-establish money supply and trade between neighboring countries. Exchange rates for the countries were set and fixed, and the US dollar was the basis for pricing in many widely needed commodities such as grains and oil.

Since the countries needed to convert their currency into dollars to purchase the needed commodities, they would need to know the exchange rate. The exchange rate for the USD was set, along with the price of 1 ounce of gold fixed at $35 USD. With this, all currencies were pegged to gold, to the dollar, and to each other.

Purchasing Power Parity

A good method that is often used to determine if a country's currency is over- or undervalued is called purchasing power parity, or PPP. It is a measurement of the misevaluation of the same goods from country to country as measured in a base currency, such as the US dollar. This PPP level is also known as the Big Mac Index, a term coined by the publishers of *The Economist*.

The Economist publishes its version of a PPP measurement by recording the cost of a McDonald's Big Mac in several countries around the world. The thought is that the Big Mac is a good measure of PPP, as it is the same commodity worldwide. If the price of a Big Mac is higher in one country than another, then that country's currency is usually overvalued against the currency of the country that sells the less expensive Big Mac.

Foreign nations could easily exchange the dollars they had in reserve for the gold held in the vaults of the US government. When the United States broke from Bretton Woods in 1971, thus effectively ending the system, the dollar was no longer convertible to gold, and with this, the "gold window" was closed. Currencies worldwide began to "float," meaning their value was determined only by supply and demand—the same way currency prices are determined today. It is often very difficult to determine if a country's currency is overvalued or undervalued against another; the currency markets tend to oscillate between overvalued and undervalued with time frames that range anywhere from several months to several years.

THE PROBLEMS WITH THE FUNDAMENTALS

While using fundamental analysis is an excellent starting point for building a case as to whether or not to build up a position in a security, such an approach has some flaws. First, the information that was used in the building of the financial analysis may not be 100 percent correct, or it may be outdated. Second, some of the key numbers used in the analysis of the security may be off, such as a company's estimated growth rate, or the estimate of a country's PPP. Lastly, even though the information related to the fundamentals and the numbers used in the estimates are true and correct, there may be a delay in when the market reacts to this information.

The combination of this misinformation, inaccurate estimates, and market delay can lead to a situation where you are building a well-thought-out position in a security and the trade fails to turn a profit or materialize in the way that you intended.

That said, even though the threat of these flaws is real, the process of fundamental analysis is often a key element in a considered day trading campaign. Reading the fundamentals, searching for trading ideas, and then switching to reading the charts in an effort to look for setups is the hallmark of a quality day trading business.

This process of starting with the big picture, looking at a country's economy, a particular sector, a security, and then switching to technical analysis to make the final decision as to a possible entry and exit point is often referred to as a top-down approach. This is used by the largest and most successful investment banks and hedge funds in their pursuit of outstanding risk-adjusted returns. It leads them, and can lead you, to a more focused security selection, all the while enhancing your returns while providing a method of allowing a form of intelligence-based risk management. If you can get the hang of reading the fundamentals, you have gone a long way in increasing the enjoyment and profitability of your day trading endeavors.

TECHNICAL ANALYSIS

Charts, Waves, and Lines

The analysis of securities wouldn't be complete without the analysis of the market's technical indicators. This can be complicated for newcomers, but it's an important skill to master. Bar charts, Elliott waves, and moving average deviations also have a hand in helping you analyze the markets, look for setups, and identify the entry and exit points of a trade. Some of the indicators tell a story about the entire market, while others are sector or security specific. The addition of technical analysis to the study of the fundamentals can result in a powerful trading program.

SECURITY-TIMING APPROACH

While fundamental analysis looks at economic data, technical analysis looks at the supply and demand data as presented by indicators. Technical analysis can be used for forecasting, and if you use it in conjunction with fundamental analysis, you can have a very successful day trading business. In fact, the big investment banks use both methods. When you are looking at the big picture and using fundamentals, you are using a security-selection approach. But when you are using charts, you are using a security-timing approach.

A chart of a security represents a snapshot of the securities price and volume over time. The most useful chart is called the bar chart. You can find access to a securities bar chart on your day trading software or at any one of the commercially available sites on the Internet.

USING CHARTS

One of the best sources of charts and technical information is *BigCharts*, found at http://bigcharts.marketwatch.com/. Some day trading platforms allow you to call up charts and draw trend lines directly on the chart. When this software is available, it is often possible to place your cursor right at the point you would like to make a buy or sell order. This can help you get a visualization of where your trades are on the chart.

Charts can be adjustable as to the time frame they cover. In order to get a full viewpoint, look at a weekly chart, which shows the securities closing prices at week's end. These weekly charts usually show a history of a year or longer and are good for getting a perspective of the price history of the security. For day trading purposes, switch to hourly and fifteen-minute charts to get an up-close look at the movement of the security in a shorter interval.

Bar charts show the highest and the lowest price of the session. They also include the volume of the security during that session. Volume is a good indicator when you are looking for support and resistance levels, and breakout activity.

CHART PATTERNS AND DOW THEORY

Patterns appear in a bar chart over time, and each pattern offers different types of information. Support and resistance patterns show traders the psychology of a security's price. When you draw a line at the average bottom price and top price, you come up with the support and resistance of the security. The top line is called the support level or support line. A breakout is when the security moves above the support level. When a breakout is reached, there will be added excitement in that security, and if the breakout is reached with above-average volume, this indicates the formation of a new trend.

The resistance is the bottom line, and when the security gets to this point, traders will sell out of the security.

If there is a lot of volume at either the support or resistance, this means there are a lot of traders using this as entry and exit points. When a security travels past its support or resistance point with a lot of volume, it is thought to be a good breakout. The point of the breakout is called a pivot point and is often followed by a test of the breakout; the market rethinks the breakout, and the security falls in price.

The accelerated activity when a security reaches a support or resistance level is due to day traders all over the world drawing the same lines. Many of them have come to the same conclusions as to where those important levels are, and they are ready to react when a level is reached. Having an ascending triangle or descending triangle is when you draw a line along the top supports and along the resistances. If the lines make a wedge shape then there is a good chance that there will be a breakout in that direction. Why would the lines make a wedge? Because the supports are decreasing in value and the resistances are increasing in value.

Gaps

A gap occurs if the trading of a security opens above or below the close of the previous day's session. This is often due to the market's reaction to overnight news.

Dow theory is used to plot the future movement of a security using the Dow Jones Industrial Average and the Dow Jones Transportation Average as baselines. The basic premise of the theory, which was developed by Charles H. Dow, the founder and first editor of *The Wall Street Journal*, is that there are hourly, daily, and weekly movements in the market. If these movements are all in the same direction (that is, up or down) and there is a high volume of trading, they indicate a market trend. The trend will continue until there are clear and definitive signs that it's ended. Many technical analysts still use this theory to explain movements in the market.

ELLIOTT WAVE AND MOVING AVERAGE DEVIATION

The Elliott wave theory employs past information about a security movement to predict the security's future direction. The basis of the theory is that securities in the market have five distinct steps, and these steps form three separate waves. In a bull market, the waves move higher, culminating in a high point at wave five. (Think of it as three mountains, each one higher than the preceding one, with valleys in between, each one higher than the valley before.) In a bear market, this pattern happens in reverse.

There are flaws to the theory, similar to the flaws of the Dow theory, as there is no distinct separation of the different steps, and it is often difficult to determine a step's number in relation to the others; i.e., you might be thinking a step is number four in a series when in actuality it is number three or even number two. It can be difficult to decipher the elements of the Elliott wave theory accurately. This should not, however, prevent you in determining for yourself its value, as many professional traders rely on its indicators in their day trading strategies.

INDICATORS

There are various signs that can help you understand whether the market is moving up or down. These are called market indicators, and savvy day traders become familiar with the most important of them.

Don't be too concerned with your calculation of some of the indicators. Often, indicators such as a two-hundred-day moving average can be easily drawn with some of the software programs that are available. Once an indicator is drawn on a chart, the chart can be saved and refreshed at each trading session.

Forty-Week Moving Average

Many technicians refer to a securities price in relation to its forty-week moving average. The forty-week moving average number for a security is figured out by taking the security's ending price for the previous forty weeks and dividing by forty. It's a *moving* average because each week you recalculate it, adding the previous week's number and dropping the oldest number. This average has the effect of smoothing the picture of the securities closing prices. Forty-week moving averages are also known as a two-hundred-day moving averages.

Fifty-Day Moving Average

Another useful chart to look at is a security's fifty-day moving average. The measure of a security's rate of movement is called its momentum and is measured by a security's moving average deviation. This number is calculated by dividing the security's last price by its ten-week moving average. Many professional day traders use this method to analyze securities that have a tendency to be very volatile. This indicator can help you determine when a new trend is in play, when a security is overbought (too high), or oversold (too low). Fifty-day moving averages are also useful in helping you get a longer-term perspective.

The Stochastic

Another useful indicator is often referred to as a security's stochastic. This is the measurement in percentage terms of the price velocity of an individual security or market index as compared to a base index set by a technician. In other words, the upward percentage movement of the individual stock as a ratio to the market as a whole (the S&P 500). If XYZ stock went up 3 percent in one day, yet the S&P 500 Index went up 2 percent, the stochastic of the stock is (3% – 2%) / 2% = 50%, or a stochastic of 50. The higher the percentage of the stochastic, the closer that security's price is in relation to that index. A stochastic of 0 percent would indicate it is at the bottom, while a stochastic of 100 percent would indicate that the security or index was at the top of the range.

MORE INDICATORS

Other Charts, Technical Indicators, and Money Supply

Technical analysis involves reading the charts, whether bar charts or Japanese candlesticks, and adds to it the reading and interpretation of technical indicators. If by grouping several technical indicators together you come upon what seems to be a trend, and the charts and the fundamentals are all telling the same thing, then you have discovered entry and exit points in the market. This section covers some of the lesser-known indicators you can use while looking for setups for day trading.

RELATIVE STRENGTH AND JAPANESE CANDLESTICKS

The popular periodical *Investor's Business Daily* publishes the relative strength number for securities. The relative strength of a security is designed to measure a security's relative price change in the year prior compared to all other securities. A relative strength number of eighty and above is considered exceptional.

Japanese candlestick charts are read much like bar charts. The main difference with a Japanese candlestick chart is what it reports. It shows the high and low for the day, and the opening and closing price of the day. Also, there is a difference in the charts for when the price at the end of the day is lower than the price at the beginning of the day, and vice versa. This is shown in the chart by color: higher is usually a yellow or white candlestick, while lower is usually a red or orange candlestick.

There are many terms that describe the patterns that Japanese candlestick charts make; there is also a consensus among many professional traders that Japanese candlestick charts are too complicated for any serious use. If you find a charting system, ratio, or indicator too complicated, feel free to switch to a chart system or indicator you feel comfortable with. Day trading is difficult enough, and you shouldn't feel obligated to complicate it further.

TECHNICAL INDICATORS

Technical indicators are a day trader's best friend. Even though not every indicator works every time, the study of several can be very valuable.

Technical indicators are drawn from business information, investor activity, market activity, etc. Keep in mind that with technical indicators it is best to use several at once, and if they are all telling the same story, then you can consider the information to be good.

MONEY SUPPLY

The first technical indicators involve money supply. Money supply is literally a measure of the amount of money that is in circulation. This includes both paper and electronic forms of money. It represents the cash in circulation, the amount in checking and savings, and the amount in commercial paper—often referred to as M1, M2, and M3, with the lowest M number representing the most basic form of money: cash in circulation. When money supply increases through an expansionary regime of a country's treasury or central bank, there is more money available for people to use in buying things.

The money supply indicator is calculated monthly and shows a year-over-year percentage increase or decrease. This number is adjusted for the Consumer Price Index so that it takes into account the impact of inflation. The money supply indicator is calculated by starting with one hundred and adding the percent change in M2, and subtracting the percent change in the Consumer Price Index. The resulting number gives that month's money supply indicator. If the number is under one hundred, that means that the rate of the money supply is less than that of inflation. Equities' prices historically have remained flat during these times. If the situation is reversed and the money supply indicator is over one hundred, equities generally do well.

Money and Security Prices

One of the things people tend to buy when there is more money available is securities. A study in the sixty years following World War II proved that security prices go up when there is an expansionary money supply.

MORE INDICATORS

The relative value of the market as a whole can be measured by comparing the ratio of the S&P 500 average earnings per share to the percentage yield of a ninety-day US government T-bill. This indicator is called the earnings per share/T-bill yield ratio and can be calculated by dividing the twelve-month earnings per share for the index by the average price of the index. The next step is to take this number and divide it by the current yield of the ninety-day T-bill. The rule of thumb is when the EPS/T-bill yield ratio is above 1.19, it is considered an indicator to buy equities. When the ratio is below .91, it is time to sell equities (1:1.19 and 1:.91 ratios intuitively, but reported as only "1.19" or ".91" etc.).

Another indicator is called the short interest indicator. Markets across the United States usually make a statement in the middle of each month reporting on the amount of short interest. This report shows the amount of shares that are held on the short sale side of investors and traders. Not only does this number represent how many people are of the mind-set that the stock market will go down, but it also shows the amount of buying power the market has at the time. The indicator is reported as a ratio or the short interest over the average daily volume of the market. An indicator below 1:0 is considered a bearish indicator, and a ratio of 2:0 or higher has historically been considered an indicator to buy equities.

Use Many Indicators

Don't get caught up in using only one or two indicators in your technical analysis of the markets or securities. It is best to instead use a handful of indicators along with bar charts and fundamental analysis to reach your conclusions about the market.

THE CBOE VOLATILITY INDEX

Another measure of the trader's nervousness and subsequent market sensitivity is the CBOE Volatility Index, also known as the VIX Index. It is an intraday index and is mainly useful as an indicator of traders' and investors' feelings about the market. The higher the VIX number is, the greater the negative feelings in the market. A normal reading is anywhere from 15 to 25. During the worst trading days of the banking crisis of 2008–2009, the number jumped as high as 80, showing a high degree of emotional turmoil and even panic in the markets. During the calm upward-moving markets of the latest bull market of 2014–2017 the VIX indicator has hovered around 12–18, sometimes falling to 10 or less for weeks on end.

MARKET BREADTH, OSCILLATORS, AND OTHERS

The Arms Index attempts to read the conditions of the stock market by looking at the number of shares on the NYSE that have fallen and risen and the volume of these shares. A number of less than 1.0 indicates that there are a lot of buyers, and a number greater than 1.0 says there are a lot of sellers in the market. A more accurate reading of this indicator is to use the ten-day moving average of the Arms Index.

There are other indicators, such as odd-lot indicators, cash holding of mutual funds, the margin amounts of retail customer's accounts, and the insider buying and selling of stock by company executives. If you start with a top-down approach and use fundamental analysis to select a country, market, sector, and then security, you can couple this information with technical analysis.

What Do Overbought and Oversold Mean?

When technical analysts refer to a security as being overbought, it usually refers to the fact that the security has risen in price too quickly and runs the chance of falling in price in the near future. The opposite is true for oversold; the security has fallen too quickly and will soon rebound.

Chapter 8

Advanced Day Trading

Once you get going with basic day trading, you can develop your craft further. You can use tighter trade setup goals, switch to trade markets you're not used to, or even train yourself to trade only on days when the picking and profit is easy. The theories of day trading remain the same, but you will apply them with a higher level of skill. This chapter will help you develop those skills and will enrich your learning further.

LOOKING FOR TRADES

Setups for Higher Returns

One of the most important sayings in trading is "Make money by sitting on your hands." This adage refers to the fact that often traders lose money by reckless trading. Even though you may not have a full-service broker and the structure of your account may only allow very low commissions, you can buy and sell too often without thinking through the trades. Worse yet, you may trade out of boredom or a desire to gain excitement through day trading. Entering into the markets to trade without looking for setups is the quickest way to end your day trading career.

SEARCH FOR SETUPS

There are two things that are essential to a profitable day trading session: good setups and free capital to commit to the trades. If your money and margin are tied up in a grouping of positions that weren't thought out but that were entered into haphazardly, you are running the risk of tying up that capital and margin, possibly in losing positions. Your goal is to preserve your capital first, and to have winning trades and to make money second, not to trade for excitement or for an experiment. If you go about day trading in the right way, you will have available cash and margin always waiting on the sidelines, always available to enter into a good setup when one becomes available. Always look for the best play of the day before you enter into a trade.

RECOGNIZING DAYS OFF

Sometimes this means the market is flat, sideways, or otherwise not giving any good indicators as to good setups. On these days it is best to continue to be "at work" but not day trade. Use those days to review your past trades, with a casual following of the markets. Sometimes, if there are no setups at the early part of the markets opening, seasoned day traders will take the rest of the day off. Their logic is that money that is not lost in bad trades or otherwise used on a flat or bad market day will be there for the next trading session. It is all right to not trade during these kinds of market sessions. You're not required to trade each day, and the markets will be there when you come back. There are some traders who stay out of the market for weeks on end, all the while checking into the charts and news looking for setups, while their cash sits on the sidelines, earning interest. These traders trade less frequently since they are looking for bigger gains with larger amounts of committed capital.

Learning to cruise for setups will go a long way in keeping your account's profit and loss statement positive. There are actually fewer times to make really good trades, get in, get out, and make a low-risk profit than there are times in which capital can be tied up in flat markets, or worse yet, unprofitable trades. Trading is a lot like fishing with more than one pole. You bait your poles, put them in the pole holders, and sit at the shore, waiting for a bite. As long as you are searching for setups, you are profitable. Only enter into trades that have good setups brewing, ones that are leading quickly to a profitable situation.

At first, sitting on the sidelines will seem unproductive, but with time and experience you will see that many of the lower-end, lower-yielding trades go nowhere, never develop into a profit, or end up being losses. It can be a good training aid to trade in your practice demo account when you encounter lower-end trades in a sideways market. This will help satisfy your desire to trade and at the same time give you a chance to learn with a "what-if" scenario.

SWITCHING MARKETS TO GET REFRESHED

You will find it helpful to switch the markets that you scan for trades once every two or three months. This will allow your mind to view new patterns and to study new trends, which can be very refreshing. Most people have a tendency to rotate among the same two or three securities looking for setups. You might have your favorite currency pair, ETF, or commodity.

After you have been in the markets for a while, you may suffer from a typical trader's problem: boredom. You find yourself looking for something different from day trading your usual securities. It is common for people who get to this point in their trading careers to want the feelings of excitement they had when trading was new.

Unfortunately, they sometimes try to rekindle those feelings by increasing the risks they take, and in particular by increasing the leverage of their trades. If you find yourself starting to think this way, it's best to switch among sectors or within sectors to trade. This will once again give you the feelings of excitement. Start day trading commodity futures after you've been trading commodity ETFs. Or explore currency pairs with different fundamentals than those with which you are familiar.

There are other ways to keep fresh, such as looking at different sources of day trading information, subscribing to new newsletters, or even switching the periodicals that you read. Another method of staying fresh with your day trading perspective is to take a month off.

It is often the feeling of being comfortable that allows you to become complacent with your risk management. If you go on a vacation with some of the money you have built up in your account, you may come back with a feeling of having splurged; this alone is often enough to make you take less risk and work harder to make profitable trades. Believe it or not, enjoying the money that you have built up in your day trading account is just as important as building up the account in the first place!

Thrill Seeker or Trader?

Are you a thrill seeker, or do you just enjoy day trading? Thrill seekers enjoy taking risk. They will seek out the good feeling they get by taking risks and will often put themselves and others at risk because of their need for thrills. Enjoying trading, on the other hand, means you take calculated risks and have a respect for the markets.

TRADING ENTRY POINTS

Using the Pyramid System

As discussed earlier, the pyramid system is a method of separating your trades into three periods, thereby in theory giving yourself three different price levels. It is similar to the dollar cost averaging theory of investing, but each of the three trades is on the books separately, instead of being grouped together.

DECIDING ON TRADES

To use the pyramid system effectively, you must first identify a potential trade. Second, go through your risk management calculation to determine the total position size that would be appropriate for your account. Then divide this dollar amount into three trades spread out during the course of the holding period. If you are buying an ETF and you determine that the trade setup will last only a few hours, a one-third entry point would be made at your initial indication to start buying into the position. If you are trading DIA (the symbol for the Dow Diamonds Trust ETF) and you determine you'd like to start buying at 130, you would buy one-third of the total calculated trade amount at this price.

As the price of DIA moves with the up-and-down movement of the Dow 30, make another one-third buy-in at a price that appears favorable. Since the Dow 30 may be moving upward during the trading period, the second and third buy-ins don't have to be at a lower price than the first one. The system is intended to spread out your entry points if the security falls in value, allowing you to have additional capital to invest at the lower price. Three different priced entry points will give you an extra cushion of risk management that can be very helpful in limiting your exposure to a falling market. Positions that are broken up into thirds are also easier to enter psychologically. It is easier to emotionally commit to a trade if you know that you have a cash reserve to buy in at lower prices if you misjudged the opportunity for the trade and the market moves against you.

Beware of One Big Trade

Don't eagerly jump into a setup with one big trade. With setups there is often a tug-of-war going on with the day traders across the globe, and the effect is to push the security up and down until it starts to move in one clear direction. Until that happens, stagger your entry points with the pyramid method.

CLOSING OUT TRADES

The pyramid system can also be used to close out trades. Your total position is divided into three equal parts. As the total position turns profitable, you begin to close it out in three trades. Dividing the closing out into thirds locks in your profits but at the same time allows for further growth in the gains of the trade. As the trade gains further, the second one-third would be sold off, locking in at that profit point, leaving the last third to be closed out at the next point. The combined effect of buying in thirds and selling in thirds can be a very effective risk management tool, as it spreads the cost of the trade over time and prices, acting as a smoothing agent to the overall cost basis of the position. At the same time, when it comes time to close out that position, the pyramid method will allow you to lock in your profits while providing flexibility to capture further gains in a moving market.

HOW MANY POSITIONS AT ONE TIME?

When you are just starting out, you may find it very helpful to only have between one and three positions open at one time. This is due to the fact that when you are first starting to day trade, you are learning to identify and interpret all of the market indicators that go into making successful and profitable trades. For example, you will be monitoring the short- and long-term charts and the market news while at the same time remembering the big-picture information, such as overall market trends and security and economic fundamentals.

Keeping the number of trades you have to a minimum will give you enough time to react to all of the market's developments and how they relate to your trades. At first you might find that watching the market develop and seeing it make your positions (and fortunes) go up and down is a bit thrilling and overwhelming at the same time. It takes some time to realize that it is real money in your account, just as it takes time to learn how to feel the emotions of winning and losing trades.

It often takes time to be able to comprehend all of the information on a trading screen. If you are starting out and you have too many positions open at one time, you might suffer from fatigue very quickly and have to end the trading session before the exit point of your trades. If you keep the number of trades you have open to three or less, you will also allow yourself time to analyze each trade after it has been closed out. Your goal at first should be to have enough trades and positions open to give yourself the training on multiple information inputs and situations. At the same time, you don't want to have too many things going on to the point of losing track of good trades, or worse yet, suffering from information overload.

MOVING TO MORE POSITIONS

After you have got the knack of day trading with three positions, you can gradually move to higher numbers of total positions open. Keep in mind, however, that when you have a great many trades open and you are using margin, you run the risk of the losses compounding into your margin account even faster.

For example, let's say you usually trade five currency pairs, commodities (a gold ETF), and equities (an S&P ETF). You have your currency account set to a margin of 50:1, and you are using the following risk management parameters: at 50:1 margin, total FX positions will not exceed 33 percent of available margin at the time of the trade. You trade the gold ETF and the S&P ETF in an equity day trading account with 50 percent margin max. You decide to use the additional diversification technique of trading across sectors: one-third commodities, one-third equity, and one-third FX in your total investment portfolio.

With this ratio you are able to have $4,995 in commodities (gold ETF), $4,995 in equities (S&P ETF), and $11,088.90 in each of the currency pairs or crosses per $10,000 in your total day trading account.

This is an illustration of how your accounts would be using margin, and the dollar amount of each position:

Gold ETF 33.3% × 1.5 margin × $10,000 total day trading account = $4,995

S&P ETF 33.3% × 1.5 margin × $10,000 = $4,995

FX Pair 33.3% × 50:1 margin × 33.33% total FX margin available = $11,088.90

MORE RISK MANAGEMENT TECHNIQUES

Managing Risk with Margin

Minimizing the risk in your portfolio can get pretty sophisticated. At the highest end, your risk management is called "hedging the risk" of your portfolio. Real hedging is getting to the point that your portfolio can withstand downside risk while still being set up to capture gains in the market. This section covers further risk management and trade hedging.

DIVIDING POSITIONS

A further risk management technique involves dividing the market long, short, and neutral positions into further thirds. One-third goes into a bucket of market long positions: long S&P ETF positions, long AUD/JPY, AUD/USD, and USD/SEK positions, etc. One-third goes into market short positions: long gold ETFs, short AUD/JPY, short USD/SEK, etc.

Go Short on Gold?

Remember, gold goes up when the markets get rough, or worse, when there is panic in the markets. Should gold be shorted? Good question. It is much easier to think of gold as a "safe haven" bet and use it as a form of a hedge against a downward-moving market. It's easy to get caught in the up and down of trades. With this in mind, think of gold as a trade you can have to make money in bad markets.

The last third is in market neutral positions, such as the soft commodities and grains, and the FX pairs with a market neutral bias (EUR/SEK, EUR/CHF, EUR/NOK, AUD/NZD, and USD/SGD). This would be for further diversifications. As you see, there are basically three markets: market long, market short, and market neutral. Within those three market "directions" there is further position diversification. Remember, diversify, diversify, diversify!

Additional risk management could be the purchase of an alternative investment mutual fund that uses a market neutral global macro style, such as UBS's Dynamic Alpha (BNACX). Dynamic Alpha is a mutual fund that is managed as a hedge fund and has extensive use of derivative overlays to neutralize risk and give a market neutral bias. Consider the addition of an alternative investment fund as a buffer in your overall day trading account, acting to further smooth out peak highs and lows due to concentrated positions. A position in a market neutral alternative hedge fund–styled mutual fund would be held for the medium-longer term, and consist of around 10 percent of your total portfolio. This 10 percent will act as a medium-term hedge to your total medium-term trading goals. Remember, while you are day trading daily, there will be ups and downs day to day in your account and even ups and downs month to month. This 10 percent will act as a diversification tool; professional traders use it as an anchor in their account, spreading the risk and diversifying even further.

PROFITS, LOSSES, AND YOUR BUYING POWER

The total buying power in your accounts will be constantly changing, moving up and down as the value of the trades in your account moves with the market. With higher-leveraged trades such as futures, commodities, or FX, your total buying power will be affected greatly by the number of open positions in your account and how well they are doing. When you first buy or sell a position to open, you are committing cash and margin to the trade. When the trade becomes profitable, more margin will be added to your account in proportion to the amount that the trade is in the profit zone.

The gain in a trade actually allows you to buy or sell more positions to the open with the additional margin created with the gains. To review, margin is used to buy a position to the open; as it moves into a profitable position, the gains are added to your account (unrealized gains). Since your account's value is higher, additional margin is available, and therefore additional buying power.

USING A HIGH RATE OF MARGIN

If you are using a high rate of margin in an FX or futures account, the gains you make will mean even more margin on the available buying power. Example: you have $10,000 in an FX account. One of your trades used $2,000 in margin, and at 50:1 the position has a total value of $100,000. As the trade becomes profitable, the gains are added to your account as more margin. If you made 2 percent on the trade, the gains would be $2,000, and this would be added to your account. This fresh $2,000 can then be spent on an additional trade at 50:1 or another FX trade with a value of $100,000. The process can be repeated with each trade's gain until you have huge positions built upon higher and higher leverage.

Eventually you can get to the point that your account has multiple positions all built on the gains of the trade before them. But the problem with this trading philosophy and style is that along with higher margin, you're amplifying the risk. If the profits in percentages and dollar amounts using the multiple leverage method have been impressive, the losses in the account can be equally impressive and equally dramatic if the market turns against you.

As the prices of the FX trades come down, any positions you have open will unwind rapidly. Your account can collapse under the weight of its own leverage. This is essentially what happens to some major hedge funds and other major financial institutions when there is a shortcoming in the risk management departments. It is a form of maximum profit generation, and when done right for short times (often through automation), it can lead to very high returns. But it can also lead to an account's rapid destruction.

PROGRAMMING YOUR TRADES FOR ENTRY POINTS

Searching for Setups

After you have mastered the art of looking for setups, and manually entering into trades, the next thing to master is programming entry points into your trading software. This automates the trading process and allows you to be a bit more hands-free on your trade entry during a trading session. You still look for setups by listening to the news, reading the journals, analyzing the fundamentals, and looking at the technical indicators.

ENTERING IN AUTOMATED TRADES

Once you have determined that a security is good to trade and has the potential to be profitable, you must determine a good entry point. Before this, you were making market orders; in other words, you were entering in the trades at whatever point the market was at the time.

When you program your trading platform to limit orders to open, what you are doing is only committing to the trade when the security reaches the price you've set or better. You can analyze the price of the security ahead of time and determine the best price to enter in order to make the highest return. If an ETF is at $48 and you determine that you would like to buy three hundred shares at $46.25 or better, you enter in a buy limit order at this price. The trading software tells your broker that the order is outstanding and in place.

When the ETF reaches this price, your order will be executed automatically, even if you are not at your day trading desk that session.

Setting the Time

When you program your trading platform with automated entry points, you can set the length of time for which you would like the order to stand. For example, you can have the order be good for the week; if by the end of the week the order is not filled, the order is automatically canceled. "Order filled" means when you place the trade on your screen, the brokerage house "officially" makes the trade for you, and therefore the ETF, stock, or FX pair is in your account—i.e., you own the trade. There is a chance that the trade won't be filled though; for instance, if the trade was placed at the very end of the day, and the market was closing. This actually happens often, as there can be quite a lot of trading activity at the last few seconds of the trading day. If you are trying to close out and sell out all of your trades in the last moments of the day, they may not all get filled.

You can couple the automatic order entry with the automatic closing-out function of your trading platform. For example, you can enter in a buy order at $46.25 and a sell order at $48.25; this order will be activated once the stock or security reaches that price—i.e., the trade will fire off and be filled automatically and will remain active unless the order is closed out manually or canceled. While it is best to remain as hands-on as possible with your analysis, looking for setups and day trading, it is possible to automate some of the process. While you can automate the actual entering and exiting of the trades, it should be your own thoughts as to when and what to buy or sell in your account. Some platforms (especially Forex) offer fully automatic trading. These are called bots or robots and can be purchased for $100–$500. They are usually well-written algorithms that upload directly into your FX platform. They are set to run fully or partially automatic and are programmed to read technical indicators to decide where to place trades. While they are interesting, and sometimes very compelling in their full automation, it is best to leave the fully auto off. If you'd like to use one, use it for suggesting trades. This way you can get to know how to read technical charts for trade setups, and you can follow along with what the robot is seeing in the charts. This way you can learn with an active market and an active computer helping you indicate when a good trade might be present. Ultimately, it's best if you decide what to trade and when.

There are plenty of companies that promise great returns by offering the use of their proprietary signal service that tells you what and when to day trade. Your goal is to own your account, and to own your day trading profits and losses. It is only when you are making the decisions for your account that you will be able to make a living, day trade as a profession, and day trade for your own profits.

PRESET PROFIT POINTS

Using Stops Effectively

An important component of automated trading is the proper use of stops. A stop is an automated sell order that is programmed into your trading platform at the time of the trade's placement. An account's risk can be measured in the percentage that the stops are placed behind the entry price. For example, if you enter into the ETF QQQQ (the Nasdaq 100 Trust) at $50 and you place the stop for that trade at $45, the stop will automatically sell QQQQ when it gets to $45, limiting your loss on the trade to $5, or 10 percent.

Lose or Gain Money?

Won't the placement of stop losses make me lose money? Stop losses do the exact opposite. While it may look as though you are selling out of your position at a loss and losing money, the real purpose of the stop is to prevent you from losing even greater amounts of money if the position moves against you by a large percentage.

If you place all of your stops at 10 percent below the entry price of your trades, you are, in effect, limiting the loss of your trades to 10 percent across the board. If you are using 100 percent of your tradable assets and you only have ten positions, you will zero out your account after ten losing trades in a row. For example, you have a $1 million account with ten trades each of $100,000 in value. If you place the stops at 10 percent behind the entry price, your trading platform will automatically sell out the positions with a $10,000 loss. If all ten trades went bad and were automatically closed out, the total loss would be $100,000 × 10 percent = $10,000 × 10 trades = $100,000 loss in total. As you can see, this $100,000 loss is 10 percent of the total fund. You are limiting your total losses to 10 percent of each trade with this system. If you continued along with these position sizes (100 percent of the account with ten trades total), you would have to lose more than one hundred trades in a row to zero out your account (this does not include the trading costs).

The use of stop losses is a form of defensive risk management. An offensive-orientated risk management technique is to program your trading platform to automatically sell your positions at a predetermined profit point. This will lock in your gain and help you plan how much you would like to make from each trade. For example, you could program your trading platform to automatically sell a security at a price that is 10 percent above the entry point. This price can be programmed in as a percentage or dollar amount before the trade is actually placed. The fields in the order entry window of your trading platform would be filled out as to dollar amount or percentage of gain, and you would then place the trade and wait for the automated sale at the profit point.

RUN THE BUSINESS LIKE A CASINO

Here is some food for thought: if you believe that the markets are completely random, are volatile, and are affected by many, many factors, make it your philosophy to run your day trading business like a casino. Casinos make money by stacking the odds in favor of the house. If a game table has a 2:3 odds, the gambler will win twice for every time the house wins three times. If you think of yourself as the "house" and if you believe that the markets are totally random and a game of chance (which some believe the markets are), you can set all of your trade stops to any odds you like. If you wanted 2:3 odds, you would set your stops to a ratio of 2:3 with the higher being the take-profit order.

For example, you could buy QQQQ at $50, set your stop loss at 4 percent behind the entry price, and your take profit at 6 percent above the entry price (2:3 ratio). If the market is totally random, you will average an automatic 2 percent on every trade (lose 4 percent, gain 6 percent, equals 2 percent net gain). In order to get this system of randomness to work properly, you have to enter many trades to get the averages to smooth out. This is a good experiment to set up in a dedicated practice/demo account.

EMOTIONS AND TRADING

Mastering Your Feelings

After you have been day trading for a while, you will feel the full emotions of winning and losing money in the markets. If you learn how to master these emotions, you can take advantage of other traders' feelings about the market. You shouldn't, however, day trade when the market upsets you, as this will cloud your judgment. You should understand how to balance risk and reward and how to know and manage your risk limits.

THE EMOTIONS OF WINNING AND LOSING

Money made in the market can give you a feeling of empowerment, a feeling of being wide awake and in control. It is a form of alchemy in a way: you are using your mental energy, intelligence, and the electric power of your computer to make money multiply.

Most of your trades will be well thought out and planned, and occasionally some of them will yield very high returns. These high-yielding returns are the positions that have a magical quality—you planned them, but they worked out better than you imagined. Once one of these trades has gone a full turn (trade opening, gain, closing, and realization of the profit), you will most likely be bitten by the day trading bug and the seemingly effortless way in which you made money.

THE THRILL OF SUCCESS

It often feels as though the gains you make in the market are making something from nothing. This is why some traders at the big investment banks are referred to as Masters of the Universe.

Not a Capital Gain

Money that is made from day trading is technically not a capital gain. For income tax purposes, money made from trading is categorized as ordinary income. This is because when a security has a round trip (the opening, holding, and closing of a position) of less than one year, it is considered short term, and therefore considered income.

However, you should remember that although your trades are based upon your planning, knowledge, and intelligence, there is a certain part of each trade that is based upon unpredictable market factors. If you keep that in mind, you will be well on your way to having a successful day trading business, and not be trading for emotional gains.

Granted, there are a lot of good emotions that come from day trading and making money; these should keep you trading, but they should not cloud your judgment with an inflated ego and the pursuit of higher and higher risk levels. This is precisely why I recommend that after a big session day trading in the markets you should walk away from your trading terminal.

Just as your emotions can be really high after making a big winning trade, they can be equally as low after a big loss, or a series of bad trades that draws your account down. If you have been following some risk management procedures such as using stops, pyramiding, and limiting position size, you should be able to walk away from a series of bad trades with more bad feelings than lost money. To go further with this thought, if you have been day trading with money that has been set aside for this purpose and have not been using money needed for necessities such as rent, etc., then your low emotional state should outweigh your lost economic status.

Emotions are the name of the game with day trading. Your goal is to think as coolly and as businesslike as possible with day trading while at the same time allowing yourself to feel the highs and lows of winning and losing in the market.

DO THE OPPOSITE OF WHAT YOU FEEL

One of the key parts of trading like a professional is learning how to think logically when emotions are running high. In some situations you know what needs to be done with a trade, but your gut is telling you the opposite. If you can coldly separate your emotions from what you have learned and have been trained to do, you can enter into very unruly markets and gain from them.

For example, in the spring of 2009 the S&P fell several percentages for a few days during a time of extreme market duress and bad banking crisis news. Most traders and investors were pulling money out of almost all sectors at the same time, which left a very precarious situation of rapidly falling worldwide markets. If you were a day trader at this time, you might have been very emotionally motivated to keep your account safely parked in cash (and even then you would be worried about the safety of your balance!). If you were thinking logically and were willing to take a small measured risk, you could have placed a small amount of your account in a highly leveraged long S&P future.

In this instance, the S&P turned around dramatically and gained more than 10 percent in one session. This would have realized you a heavy gain if you'd done the opposite of how you *felt* the market was reacting. This is an extreme case, but many professional traders will tell you that the market often sends out very negative signals just before the best setups happen and profits are to be made.

Trust Your Training

Often, doing the opposite of what you feel means doing what you have been trained for and what is logically right. If you know that markets are reactionary and emotional in nature, you can learn to exploit the negative emotions that often run in the world of trading. Two of the most common negative emotions are fear and greed. Fear is the emotion that you will lose your money in bad market conditions, and greed is that you will lose out on a perceived gain by remaining in the markets past the normal growth of a position. Using logic and going against the normal feelings you have can guide your day trading to strong returns. You should be as logical and as opportunistic as possible with the appropriate risk management procedures in place.

Some of the large investment banks and hedge funds throughout the world are using this method to the extreme—they attempt to use computer programming and automation to predict outcomes and execute orders using statistics, higher mathematics, and mathematical logic. While these are extreme cases, you can take a cue from some of these methods. To apply pure logic to an emotional animal such as the world's markets and do so with a cool conviction can be a very difficult task. If mastered, the effects on your trading account's profits can be very dramatic!

TRADE WHAT'S HOT

Listening to the Market

You will grow your skills by listening to the market. There are different sources for getting information about the market. How much information, the source of the information, and the quality of the information are some of the questions you should be asking. Whether it is from your broker, television, or the Internet, you should ask yourself, *Does this information help me decide what, when, and how much to day trade?*

EVERYONE'S TELLING YOU WHAT TO TRADE

With finance, the markets, and day trading, there are often a lot of people telling you what you should do. It is good to remember this because market movement prediction and economics are not absolute sciences, and there can be a lot of different ideas and opinions as to what's the best view of the market.

Learn to be choosy as to whom you will accept as your information source. You will naturally think of economics and the market all of the time when the market is really hot and you are trading day in and day out. Your goal should be to get yourself to the point where you are the expert. When reading *The Wall Street Journal*, watching CNBC, and consulting your broker's reports, you must get to the point when you are scanning for a key bit of information that you can use as a trading idea.

Pressure

Brokerage firms are known to place tremendous pressure on their brokers to get clients. Some firms have training programs that have quotas of $1 million a month in new, investable assets over a two-year period. These brokers will be very eager to land your account. You should proceed with caution when dealing with these types of firms.

CONSIDERING EMOTIONS

Remember, you are dealing with the markets: most information sources deal in facts and logic, but the market is an illogical animal. This is because all of the investors and traders are dealing with money; along with this money comes emotions of fear and greed. The herd mentality, coupled with the fact that most players in the market are, in a way, placing educated bets, leads to emotional and illogical markets. It helps to think like a professional gambler, with the markets as your huge, worldwide casino. The casino of the markets has so many variables that it is foolish to think that an information source can predict them all. This is what the big quantitative hedge funds and trading desks of investment banks attempt to do: the application of logic, statistics, and mathematics to unpredictable markets that are driven by emotion. When you think of yourself as truly an independent day trader, you will pull yourself away from the information and view it as all noise, but also as an inside view into what the other market players are thinking and feeling.

QUESTIONS TO CONSIDER

When you hear someone talking about the market (or money in general), ask yourself what her motivation is:

- Is the person on the news really convinced that what he is saying is true, or is he just making a statement to fill time on the air?
- Is the article in the magazine really that important, or does that magazine need to have that many pages and the publisher fills it with fluff?
- Is this person overall negative in nature because he had a bad experience, and does this mean you will have the same experience?
- How much of the report you are reading is based upon fact?
- Can this be true?
- What is the researcher's track record?
- Should you or shouldn't you care what the market thinks?

If you were a contactor buying supplies and hiring subcontractors for your building project, would you take any plan that was given to you? Would you pick up wood and nails off the street, even if they were free for the taking? Would you ask a dentist to approve the quality of your supplies? The best thing to remember is that it's your money. Have confidence with your views, and be selective with the information you believe.

ADVANCED RISK

Risk versus Rewards

It is often said that you must assume risk to get a reward. This statement is only partially true. It leaves out the fact that there is a limit to the amount of return that can be gained from a unit of risk, and that often, with diversification, you can reduce risk while enhancing returns. This concept of limiting risk and enhancing reward is called modern portfolio theory. It was first introduced by Harry Markowitz in his 1952 paper "Portfolio Selection," in which he mathematically proved that risk could be reduced by the movement away from single securities and toward the inclusion of noncorrelated securities into the portfolio. By correlation he meant when different market sectors or individual stocks or other financial products all move up together at the same percentage or all down together at the same percentage. Markowitz designated the degree of correlation by the Greek letter beta. A security whose movement was 100 percent in tandem with the rest of the market has a beta score of 1.0. One that moves only half as much as the market has a score of 0.5; one that moves at twice the market average has a score of 2.0.

Modern Portfolio Theory

Modern portfolio theory (MPT) is based on many assumptions: one of these is that the correlations among assets will be fixed and constant forever. This part of MPT was challenged during the banking crisis of 2008–2009 when most of the world's markets and asset classes' betas became correlated with each other, causing many traders and investors to hold undiversified portfolios.

VOLATILITY REDUCTION

Think of your overall account value, i.e., all of your accounts with all brokerages, as one big portfolio. In your overall portfolio, you can make the addition of lower beta securities and still obtain a high level of potential return in your accounts. Your positions might include an S&P 500 position, commodities, market sensitive FX positions, and market neutral FX positions. Using different layers of risk "buckets" measured in beta, you can build an overall portfolio that would include high risk, high return, high beta positions; medium risk, medium beta positions; and lower risk, lower beta positions. Using a bit of math, you can calculate your overall account's beta to arrive at a number. The goal is to have a desired potential return while having a beta of 1.0 or less. This would mean that your risk was at the same level as trading an S&P 500 position (often referred to as "the overall market").

The difficulty comes in arriving at a realistic beta measure of any one of your positions. The beta of equities and ETFs are found easily on finance websites; others can take a bit of research and work, but betas can be estimated via proxy. For example, you can derive the beta of a currency pair in an FX or futures trade by looking up the beta of some of the currency ETFs that are available to trade. After a bit of practice, you can also make educated estimates for the other sectors. Some sophisticated trading subscription services offer the beta of most every tradable asset and sector available.

KNOW YOUR RISK LIMITS

When you are setting up a portfolio of positions or placing an individual trade, it is important to know your individual risk tolerance. If you are starting to learn how to day trade, you might want to "detune" your strategies and only enter into trades that are lower risk.

When you are just starting out, it is important to have adequate time to develop positions and not to have too many fast-moving, volatile, and risky trades open. This will give you more mental room to think about how each trade is reacting to the market's news and other developments.

Limiting Your Risk

Limiting the risk in your day trading sessions can be as easy as using less of your overall portfolio's cash balance, day trading three uncorrelated asset classes, or even limiting your trading times to sessions when only long positions will be profitable.

Keeping your trades simple and being more risk averse will make each of your day trading sessions move slower; it will tend to bring more comfort and enjoyment to your day trading business. Day trading with real money in fast-moving markets is stressful and filled with pressure. If you can learn to ease these factors by limiting your risk, you are going a long way in keeping your day trading sessions positive experiences, ones from which you can learn and build on. Don't feel as though you have to be trading with high levels of margin, with unfamiliar sectors, or with high dollar amounts. If you feel comfortable starting with minimal risk at the cost of smaller returns, then this system is good for you. Once you get the gist of analyzing market news, studying the fundamentals, reading the charts, and day trading successfully, it is easy to search for higher returns by increasing your risk appetite.

Higher risk can be accepted into your portfolio when you are ready: you might start with higher dollar amount trades, multiple trades at the same time, or more complicated trading techniques.

YOUR RISK TOLERANCE

The key is to know your risk tolerance and stay within those boundaries. No one should force you to take on too much risk if it makes you feel uncomfortable. You might be 100 percent fine with day trading equities and ETFs. In fact, you might be so pleased with your returns for the amount of risk you are taking that you may never want to venture into the world of commodities, futures, or FX.

Don't start to think that you are not a real day trader just because you have adjusted your risk level to the point that you are enjoying your business, making money, and generally pleased with your results. Just because others seem to be suffering with their day trading efforts doesn't mean that they are more of a day trader than you. It may, in fact, be that the others who are having problems are expecting too much out of day trading; they may be trying complicated prepackaged commercial systems or to squeeze too much profit out of too small an account.

Day trading should enhance your life, give you enjoyment, intellectual stimulation, and profit. It should not turn your world into a complicated mess of struggling with placing trades and then worrying about the potential effect on your account (and mental well-being!). Keep it small and simple, and then if you would like, build up into a more risk-oriented structure in your account.

QUICK TRADING

Scalping and Swatting

There are different types of day trading: all are designed to make a profit, but differ in the length of time each trade takes and how much of the account will be used. For example, scalping is a trading technique of moving small amounts of money into and out of trades very quickly, with the average trade lasting ten minutes or less. It is best done with three to five positions open at any time with the aim of gently gaining little by little throughout the trading period. It can be a casual way to spend the evening, as you can trade FX on your laptop while watching the evening news. With even the smallest account balances, scalping can be fun and profitable. Commit only 5 percent or less of your total buying power to each trade; with five of six positions open, you should not exceed 33 percent of your total buying power at any one time.

Regulating Scalping

Some brokerage firms have strict guidelines as to your trading, intended to regulate the effect of very large dollar amounts of scalping. If you plan on doing any amount of this type of trading, check first with your potential broker.

You can switch from each chart showing the different securities you are watching, but make sure you are looking at very short time frame charts: check out a five-minute chart for a trend overview, then switch to fifteen or thirty seconds after you are in the trade.

HOW TO PLACE THE TRADE

The best bet is to open up the "place order" box and move it off to the side of your screen to make room for the charts. Watch the fifteen- or thirty-second chart to show that trading has slowed and that the market is taking a breather. Next, get the trade ready to go, including number of units, leverage ratio, and long or short. Put your cursor over the "place trade" button.

What you are waiting for is the security to move suddenly away from the point at which it was resting: you want to place the trade at the beginning of the movement and close out of it at the end of the movement. These will be your setups, and although most setups use fundamentals as well as technicals, you won't use them in this type of trading. You are just looking to capture the short-term movements, regardless of the overall fundamental or technical indicators. In and out within minutes with small amounts of money: it is a safe, fun, and quick way of earning extra returns for your account, and over the course of the time it takes to watch a few movies, you could add up some real earnings.

SHORT-TIME LENGTH "SQUAT" TRADES

The shorter the time length that you are actually in the trade, the lower the expected percentage movement of the security is. When you get to very short-term trades of a few minutes, securities do not have much time to move dramatically in any direction. To compensate for the small percentage movements that happen in ultra-short time frames, commit larger amounts of margin and dollars to the trades.

These ultra-short trades can be thought of as similar to a weight lifter squatting while lifting a barbell over his head. The weight lifted in a squat is very heavy, and it is hoisted over the athlete's head in a short, quick, clean jerking movement. The goal of the squat is to lift the heavy weight only once: squatting is not an endurance sport. If you have this perspective in mind, you will load on more than the usual amount of margin and money (the heavy weight) with the intention of getting out of the trade after a slight upward movement in the security. If the amount you have in the trade is large enough, you can close out the trade very quickly and still make a good profit.

It is true that this type of trading leads to a situation in which large amounts of your capital are tied up in one or two trades. This indeed goes against the usually recommended risk management techniques of using smaller amounts of capital per trade and diversification of positions across securities, sectors, and market bias.

You can use a modified form of risk management when using the high-dollar/margin trades. This risk management includes only having one or two trades open at the same time and using tight stops.

How Much of My Total Margin/Cash Should I Use on Short-Term Trades?

Your combined margin/cash amount for all of your ultra-short-term trades should be no more than one-third your total amounts of margin/cash available. If you have $10,000 in your account, have no more than $3,300 committed to anywhere from one to three positions in this type of trading.

The use of tight stops means that you've programmed your trading platform to close out the trade when the price of the security is very close to the buy-in price. Both the take-profit and the stop-loss orders are programmed in before the trade is made, and you predetermine the gains on the trade in dollar amount beforehand (after transaction costs). The dollar amounts of the gains can be very small as compared to the capital involved in the trade: what you are looking for is small, quick gains made in a time frame of five to ten minutes or less.

Markets have a way of just creeping along slowly when you are trading in these short periods. It is important that you do not take your eyes off the profit indicator of your trading platform when you are doing this kind of trading. In fact, it is recommended that you call up the close-order screen as soon as the order is opened with thoughts of closing out the trade soon thereafter. The longer the trade stays open, the more risk that other traders will force the security to move against your position. This is because trades move with time: the shorter the time in the trade, the less percentage the trade will move (and the less chance it will move against you at a loss—if a trade is open longer, there is a greater opportunity for the trade to move even more in percentage and therefore a greater chance of losing that much more). It is best to get into a trade that is moving and get out quickly. If the trade does not move, or the market is taking a breather, your best bet is to get out of the trade.

Remember, the shorter time frame of this type of trade will reduce (though not eliminate) your risk. If the trade doesn't perform in a few minutes, exit it: when you do this, the only thing you will lose is the transaction cost of the trade. This is a small price to pay for being risk averse with your account.

TRADING OVERNIGHT OR LONGER

Working in Overseas Markets

Normally with day trading, your account starts with 100 percent cash at the beginning of the trading session and is back in 100 percent cash by the end of the trading session. However, there is a different type of trading that involves the overnight markets, usually in futures and FX accounts. In order to trade overnight, look at the developments in the markets that are open on the other side of the world. US markets are usually traded in the early morning until the early afternoon.

You can get some good news and indicators as to what the developments will be in the Asian and European markets from late in the night. To trade overnight effectively, program your buy and sell orders into your trading platform in the evening. The program executes the trades automatically when the trade enters into buy or sell points while you are sleeping. Some traders make it a habit to get up early in the morning before the US markets open to see if any of their orders have been filled. If you follow this method, you can find your trades placed, with sometimes both the opening and the closing taking place, and wake up to a profit in your account.

The other variation on this method is to look at the developments of the world's stock markets for the previous few sessions and decide if the world's markets will be up, down, or sideways for the next session. You would then buy into the future or FX pair that follows the markets' risk sentiment (meaning a risk-on or a risk-off day) and place a sell order near the buy-in price. You would determine the direction of the markets by the indicators of the Asian markets, which open around seven p.m. Eastern time.

If the world's markets have been in an upward movement for a few days, and there has been a big run-up in traders' risk sentiment, then the currency pairs that follow this risk sentiment will have also been up during this time. If you check the Asian markets after a few days of the US and European markets being up, and the Nikkei (a Japanese stock market index), the Hang Seng (a Hong Kong stock market index), and others are down, there is a good chance that the world's traders are selling off some of their positions and taking their profits. You might decide to short the risky currency pairs and go long on the risk-averse pairs and commodities such as gold.

Middle-of-the-Night Trading

You might find placing trades for overnight fulfillment to be very stimulating. In fact, many day traders find themselves getting up in the middle of the night to check if their order has been filled. Better yet, some traders put their trading platforms on "audible," which allows their trading platforms to announce "order filled" when an entry is filled by the platform.

LONGER-TIME TRADES

Longer-time trades last anywhere from three days to a month. This is obviously longer than trading done in a single day, but it is covered here to help round out your knowledge of how trading works. Your knowledge of day trading wouldn't be complete without knowing the basics of longer-term trading. Remember, day trading is basically a "buy and hold" strategy, but within a few minutes or hours. Knowing how longer-term trades work will help you master short-term trading too. With this type of trading, your goal is to build up a position over time with several accumulation points. When you reach these points, you buy more of the security. For instance, you might have a simple buy-on-the-dips trading philosophy.

This is a very hands-on technique that keeps you watching your position develop. The goal is to have a selling point in mind and a value at which, when the security falls below this point, you will accumulate more, much like in the pyramid method. In this instance, though, you divide your buys into three to five prices, but when you exit, you still sell out with three equal amounts.

Set Your Stop-Loss Orders

If you are in the process of setting up a long-term trade, do not let the trade just sit on the books if it falls below a certain loss amount. Just as with any other type of trade, you should still be setting stop-loss orders to prevent a long-term position from becoming a big loser.

This longer-term trading method is good for seasonal security setups and FX carry trades. Some good targets for this longer time frame include gold futures, gold ETFs, and energy securities, all of which are good movers during the late fall and into the winter. You can accumulate the energies on particularly warm days, when the prices of heating oil and natural gas tend to move downward. This accumulation would be done with a target selling date as well as a target selling price.

DIVERSIFICATION, LEVERAGE, AND TRADING RISK

Building Uncorrelated Positions

Position building and risk management techniques go hand in hand. You can take steps to limit and control the amount of risk you are taking with each trade and each position. A popular method of building a position while limiting risk is the use of the pyramid method. After you are in the trade, effective uses of stop losses and take-profit stops will help you quantify and limit the amount of loss possible on a trade, all the while locking in the profit target of the position.

VALUING THE TRADE AND BUILDING POSITIONS

A good thing to remember when you are thinking about entering into a trade is the fact that you are buying the cheaper end of the trade. What this means is that the product you are in, whether cash, a stock, ETF, or future is more expensive than the product you are buying. For example, if you are in cash and you are thinking of buying a stock, then the cash is priced higher relative to the price of the stock. If you have a stock that you are thinking of selling, then cash is priced lower than the stock. In other words, when selling stock, cash is a better value than the stock. It is the cheaper end of the trade.

This system is a really good way to value any purchase or sale of a security. Ask yourself what's the better value, the cash or the stock (ETF, etc.). When thinking of entering into a currency pair, you should ask yourself which currency is the better value. (Or, what's cheap? What's expensive?) By answering this question, you will avoid getting into a position that is at the top of its value against what you are selling. Buying the cheaper end of the trade is a good system to help you decide if a trade is worth getting into, and deciding when to reverse the trade and go back into cash.

Which End Is Cheaper?

In order to find out which end of the trade is the cheaper one, you need to know quite a bit about security analysis, including fundamental analysis and technical analysis. Often, though, when trading a security for a long time, you will develop a gut feeling of what is the cheaper end of the trade.

LIMITING POSITION SIZE

The use of risk management can be a very effective tool to keep your account intact, even after a series of bad trades. The system that is best used is one of limiting position size, limiting concentrated positions within industry sectors, and using stops effectively. The goal of effective risk management is to develop a system of using a bit of math to get your positions built and closed in a profitable way while minimizing the chance of losing money. While the market can turn against you, and trades can go bad, you can follow some steps to limit losses.

The first method is to limit position size. This is true if you are using an equity broker, an FX broker, or a futures broker with or without margins. Think of your total amount of available trading value to be no more than 20 percent in one position. If you have an account with a $50,000 value, and you use one-half margin, you will have a buying power of $75,000. If it is your normal procedure to use 50 percent of your buying power at any one time, the total amount you can have for one position is $75,000 × 50 percent = $37,500 × 20 percent = $7,500.

Risk Management

Risk management is often one of the most misunderstood departments in an investment bank. In a big investment bank there are all sorts of traders who are building positions in their own sectors. The risk management function of the bank sometimes acts as the police, preventing any excessive buildup of a position across the company.

This 20 percent rule is a good method to force you to diversify your positions to no less than five positions at any one time. This diversification between securities will go a long way in keeping your account intact. Twenty percent is the high end of the position size rule, and a drop in the percentage to 15 percent or even 10 percent will further enhance the diversification of your day trading portfolio.

LIMIT CONCENTRATED POSITIONS

In addition to limiting position size and therefore diversifying the securities you are trading in, you should limit concentrated positions by diversifying across industry sectors, or even products. This can be achieved by bundling all of your positions in each industry, such as energy, metals, financials, retail, etc., as one position. This is done because there is a good chance that all of the securities within an industry will go up or down at the same time according to the market's movements.

If you are in three positions in the banking sector, then you would further enhance your risk management by bundling these together as one position. A second level of risk measurement would be to bundle the markets in which the securities trade, such as equities, commodities, or FX.

Remember, you are trying to get a snapshot of your overall risk and trying to quantify the overall uncorrelated diversification of your entire day trading portfolio. The uncorrelated diversification of your day trading portfolio is when you have different positions spread across many securities, industries, and markets, so that when one trade turns bad, it is supported by many others that are not related or affected by that trading/market event or news.

LEVERAGE AND TRADING RISK

Actual Returns and Potential Trades

When thinking of the returns you can accrue from day trading, it is good to keep in mind the returns from investing in the stock market over the years and the returns that you can generate by putting your money in an FDIC-insured CD. Granted, in day trading you are not investing, and you certainly are not saving, but it is good to compare the annual returns of the three. With the FDIC-insured CD, your money will be safe, but interest will creep along at a slow compounding rate. CDs usually compound once a month, meaning that the interest is added to the principal; the interest payment is recalculated after that, and so on.

CDs pay anywhere from less than a 0.1 percent to 5 percent a year depending on the interest rates of the economy. On the other hand, the historical average for keeping your money in the S&P 500 for a year is around 10 percent annually. With both of these calculations, the time length involved is a year. When you are day trading, the returns can be anywhere from 0.1 percent to over 10 percent, but the length of time that it actually takes to make the trade is often less than a day. Many times, holding the security to generate the returns may only take a few hours.

The Great Recession

In 2008 the Dow 30 fell by 34 percent, and this was its worst performing year since the Great Depression back in the early 1930s. This was due to the banking crisis of 2008–2009, a crisis that almost turned Wall Street and Main Street into a panic. If only you would have shorted the market with a 2x or 3x bear ETF!

If you are holding a security for a day and you are making 1 percent on the trade, you would annualize the returns to make a comparable against the returns for the CD and S&P 500 investment. In other words, while the trade might net 1 percent on the trade, this is for one day of trading. To annualize this, you'll need to figure out how much return you'd make if you made the 1 percent return for the whole year, just like investing in a CD and holding it for one year. In order to calculate this, multiply the return by the holding period in days multiplied by 365. If your trade was held for one day and returned 1 percent, the annualized return on the trade would be 365 percent. If you held the security for six hours (one quarter of a day), the annualized returns would be 1 percent × 4 × 365 days = 1460 percent. If you were in a carry trade that lasted one month/twelfth of a year) and your returns were 20 percent, your annualized returns would be 20 percent × 12 = 240 percent.

As you can see, the length of time that you actually hold the security determines the annualized returns. These returns are the reference required to make an accurate return-per-trade comparison to CDs and the "buy and hold" returns that are quoted by the media.

Keep in mind, though, that by no means should day trading be considered an investment: there is a considerably higher degree of risk associated with day trading and the use of leverage, but the goal is to quantify the returns on an annualized basis. Once you have the annualized returns, you are able to better compare the percentage returns your day trading is making.

In addition to the returns, once a trade is closed out and the funds are ready to trade with again, you will have a higher balance with which to trade, which also means more available margin. This has the effect of compounding your money, but the compounding is done very quickly (within the day or a few days) as opposed to compounding once every month, quarter, or year. The combined effect of the high returns matched with the frequent compounding can lead to very dramatic gains over a month or year.

SOME TRADING STRATEGIES

An appropriate overnight trading strategy would be to short AUD/JPY, EUR/SEK, and USD/SEK. These currency pairs follow the markets very closely. When the stock markets are up, they will be up; when the world's stock markets are down (when the market is said to be risk averse), they will be down. A good hedge in this scenario would be to go long on a gold future or short an S&P 500 future.

The goal is to place your trades before the traders in Europe and the United States wake up, analyze the markets, and begin to sell off, causing a lessening in risk sentiment of the markets. If you make currency trades, enter your stop loss markers and take-profit stops to trigger within a reasonable range of movement: FX trades can move as much as 0.5 percent to 1.0 percent overnight.

This seems like a small amount when compared to equities, but remember, you are using high amounts of leverage in your FX accounts: a 0.5 percent gain at 50:1 leverage will yield a gain of 25 percent on your investment. This means you will return 25 percent on the dollar for every dollar of your actual money in the trade. Overnight trading can be a profitable way to trade the equity index futures or FX, as the indicators can be easy to read through the activity of the Asian markets, before the European and US markets are even open.

POTENTIAL TRADES

If you are buying energies, the target selling price might be in mid-December, just as the temperatures start to fall in the eastern United

States. If you are accumulating gold, your selling target might be at the end of the year or even late January, as the price of gold historically moves up at the beginning of the winter and continues until the spring.

An example of an FX carry trade might be to go long AUD/JPY, AUD/USD, NZD/USD, etc., or any combination of buying a higher-yielding currency by selling a lower-yielding currency. Trades such as this allow you to accumulate the interest differential on a daily basis as well as the upward movement in price between the currencies. The interest differential in trade can add up quickly and can act as a form of downside protection in an FX trade. (The interest rate differential is the difference between the selling currency's interest rate and the buying currency's interest rate.)

This works because with FX carry trades you are borrowing in a low-yielding (low interest–charging) currency and parking the amount you have borrowed into a high-yielding (high interest-paying) currency. For example, you could borrow the USD and pay an interest rate on the borrowed amount. The interest rate on borrowed USD might be 1 percent annually. You would then move this money in AUD, a historically higher-yielding currency, and earn anywhere from 3.5 percent to 7 percent annually, depending upon the prevailing rates in Australia at the time. The rate you are earning in the carry trade is the difference between the two: AUD minus USD. If you earned 5.5 percent on the AUD and paid 1 percent on the USD, you would earn 4.5 percent annually on your trade just in interest.

Remember, you are leveraging your money anywhere from 10:1 to 500:1 in an FX account. If your leverage were 100:1, the yield on the trade would be 450 percent on the actual equity involved (the amount of actual cash put up for the trade). Not only would you enjoy the carry trade returns, interest rate is usually calculated and rolled over on a daily basis with FX accounts, even on weekends. While this book is about day trading, and that means you end the day with no trades on the books, this book wouldn't be complete without describing how interest is calculated in FX accounts. It is compounded daily, every day, weekends included.

Chapter 9

Managing Your Accounts
and Profits

After you've day traded for a while, you might want to make it a full- or part-time endeavor. Part-time day trading can be very profitable and can allow you to have a full-time regular job: this can lessen the strain on profit making, as well as giving you the chance to learn the business at a slower, more comfortable rate. Full-time trading, on the other hand, can be very lucrative and can offer you independence, much like owning your own business: you set your own hours, have financial independence, and don't answer to a boss. So, full time or part time? This chapter will help you figure out the answer to that question.

FULL TIME OR PART TIME?

Making a Commitment

Once you master the art and science of looking for trade setups, managing leverage, and getting a feel for when to enter and exit a trade, the next thing you'll need to do is decide on a plan that incorporates day trading into your lifestyle. Day trading can be done at all hours of the day, nearly six days a week, with the markets around the world providing you the chance to trade full time or part time.

DAY TRADING PART TIME

If you are looking for a more leisurely way to earn extra money, or a scaled-down approach to day trading, then you'll want to trade part time. There are many day traders who profit from day trading on a part-time basis while holding a full-time job, being a full-time parent, or are otherwise fully engaged at another activity. Day trading part time is a bit slower and often easier than full-time trading. Why? Simply because the part-time trader is less emotionally involved with his trading account, and therefore can wait it out while searching for the best trade setups. Remember, with trading it's sometimes keeping out of a bad trade that earns you the profit for the day. Staying away from the rapid-fire, got-to-trade mentality can keep your trading account profitable, intact, and not "blown up" by overprocessing and overtrading your account.

What's the best way to keep an account intact and profitable? The answer is simple: trade less, and trade more profitably.

You can be very successful and profitable with as little as five or six well-placed trades a month. If you limit your trading times to the optimum trading market environment and earn your 5–10 percent on each trade once a week, you'll be very successful indeed.

If your goal is to add to the profitability of your overall portfolio holding with only ten trades a month, with each trade being done at the perfect setup, then you could spend as little as five or ten hours a week studying the markets and looking for trades.

Less Is Best

It's a fact that most professional traders wish they would have passed on a quarter of the trades they've made on any given day, week, or month. Trades that win, win big, and it doesn't take a lot of them to keep a trading account pumping out profits. Less is best, is the saying in trading.

Part-time traders may earn a smaller percentage of overall profit in their accounts, but most often this is due to less trading, not less profitable trades. So, trading less, but earning more per trade (and risking less!) is also part of a well-thought-out part-time day trading business plan.

DAY TRADING FULL TIME

If you are looking for a career change or are looking for a work-for-yourself type of career where the potential to earn big paychecks is the norm, then day trading full time might be for you. If your account is big enough, or you are investing a sizable portion of your 401(k), inheritance, business sales proceeds, or saved moneys, then yes, day trading needs to be done full time, if only to manage all the open positions, leverage, and risk. Day trading with a big account is serious business, not only because of the money that can be made on a daily, weekly, and yearly basis; large sums of money take a bit of babysitting! Even with a semiautomated or fully automated trading strategy, it will be a full-time job to think through and calculate each trade.

Keep Your Eye on Things

Even with fully automated trading systems, expert traders never really "take their hands off the wheel"—rather, they are at their trading desks early, watching and confirming the machine's "trading logic" behind each trade...even if they themselves wrote the software!

If you decide to trade full time, it is possible to turn your hobby into a very profitable business. You will learn that much faster if you spend more time analyzing the market for trade setups, noticing innuendo in market reports that are published by brokers, and getting a grip on the world economies and how they interact on a large stage, all interconnected to each other's markets. Trading is an art as much as it is a science. You learn to do it by studying this book, going through the recommended reading list, examining brokers' reports, and yes, actually placing trades!

The more trades you enter and exit (both profitably and at a loss), the better you will become at trading. Remember: the best traders make very educated trades. These day traders execute trades that are well thought out, well planned, and have the best technical and fundamental indicators. These traders think through each trade, before, during, and exiting the trade! The most successful, enjoyable, and profitable experience is when you can use logic and art to preplan a trade, enter into it, watch it work out in your direction, exit the trade at the predetermined point, and log the profits. Remember: knowing, doing, and then realizing what you knew would happen is the most powerful edge in day trading.

To get to this point will take time as you scour the markets looking for setups, thinking, preplanning, and executing trades. It is the preplanning, then trading, and then exiting the trade at the predetermined point that makes you a professional trader. Those three habits will set you apart from other traders and day traders. The logic and the planning is as powerful, if not more so than just a few winning trades (when you can't replicate them!).

CHOOSE WHAT'S BEST FOR YOU

Day trading can be full time or part time; both types of trading plans can be profitable if you execute them well. Keep in mind the time you have available, the risk you're willing to tolerate, and the way in which day trading will work into your life situation the best. Go with that, and you won't go wrong!

REALISTICALLY LOOKING AT PROFITS

Using Your Judgment

You will know when you are ready to make your first trade when you can approach day trading as a business that you find very enjoyable, exciting, and profitable. Of these three, first and foremost day trading should be enjoyable. When you look at it that way you can move away from constantly looking for the profit rush, a feeling of euphoria that comes about when a profit is made in the markets. This profit euphoria can be addicting, and it can lead a day trader to take on greater and greater risks or position sizes in search of greater and greater gains. Be careful of these feelings!

EVERY TRADER HAS BAD DAYS

Even hardened traders have bad days. They are armed with their best judgment, but sometimes the market goes against them. When this happens, they sit back and evaluate the risk level of every position they are in. Keep this in mind when you get the urge to increase the risk in your account. This mentality can be destructive to your profit and loss statement. There is only so much profit that you can squeeze out of an account. In order to exceed this natural profit amount, it is necessary to take bigger risks through larger margins, concentrated positions, etc. This is not good business and not a way to turn your day trading into a career. You should learn to start small, manage risks, limit margin, and know your profit and loss points all with the thought of learning to day trade better.

In trading careers, there is no "one big trade." That is stuff of Hollywood and fantasy. In order to make a living at day trading, you must make small, measured profits day in and day out. If you consistently make more winning trades than losing trades at the end of the day, your account will show an overall profit. This should be your second goal.

The last goal should be excitement. You will learn that this excitement comes naturally whenever you are dealing with money and the markets. It can be thrilling to day trade.

Mastering a sector, knowing a product, following it in the news, and then making money by day trading the product you know so much about can be very fun and satisfying. This is a measure of how well you are taking to your new business of day trading. If at any time you do not feel the same excitement making regular, risk-managed, relatively safe trades, and you want to thrill seek by changing margin ratios, taking bigger bites of a position than you are used to, or getting into exotic products, take a break. When you start having these feelings, you are taking your successes and profits for granted.

So take a few weeks off. Withdraw some of the money in your account and buy something fun, or take the family on a vacation. In this way you will get some use out of the money you would probably lose if you started to take increased risks before you were ready.

ARE YOU READY?

Finally, you will ask yourself, *Am I ready to make my first trade?* You will never be able to answer this question fully without the acceptance of some risk. Not every day trading opportunity offers the perfect chance to make money. Day trading is not an absolute science. If you have been studying the fundamentals, watching the markets, and reading the charts, then you are ready to trade. Starting with small dollar and margin amounts will take the pressure off of your first series of trades and will allow you to get into the markets sooner rather than later.

Checklist for Your First Trade

- Read your broker's overall market reports
- Check the daily market news
- Monitor the long and medium time frame charts
- Watch the trends
- Plan your entry and exit points
- Place the trade

It is important to try to make your first day trading experiences positive ones. Starting small and getting out of the trades early with even the smallest amount of profit will enable you to have the experience of enjoying day trading on your terms.

Rather than jumping into a live account, practice first. Much money can be lost in the first few days of day trading if you are not 100 percent fully ready for the action, excitement, and pressure that it takes for day trade with a live account. Keep your money safe for as long as possible and day trade in your demo account for a while. Remember, you're taking a long view of day trading, giving yourself the best chance to make profitable trades. If you try too hard and place too many big trades without sufficient experience, these trades could well result in rapid losses from your account. If you aren't patient during your first few trades, then you will set a pattern of approaching your day trading sessions in a state of tension, frustration, or worse yet, panic.

BUILDING YOUR ACCOUNT SLOWLY

The Mathematics of Returns

When calculating returns you have to look at the core dollar amount that is in your profit and loss for the days, weeks, and months, and from this figure a monthly or quarterly average. The reason you look at your returns on a daily basis is that in annualized percentage terms, you might have stellar performance in your day trading account.

If, for example, you are in a trade that returns 2 percent of the dollar amount, at first glance it might seem small. When you annualize the returns, the numbers can change dramatically due to the ultra-short holding time of day trades.

If you are to calculate the annual returns on the 2 percent gain, take the 2 percent daily return and multiply it by the number of days in the year, 365 = 730 percent annualized returns. To dig even deeper, take the return percent for the trade, divide it by the number of hours' holding time of the trade (let's say three hours), multiply this number by twenty-four hours in a day, and multiply this number by the number of days in a year (365). Two percent divided by three hours = 0.667 percent, multiplied by twenty-four hours = 16 percent, multiplied by 365 days = 5840 percent annualized returns when calculated on an hourly holding period.

Although this is a not a standard method of calculating returns, it provides a means of comparison even if the returns on the CD are compounded monthly rather than annually.

Bank's Calculation of Returns

Banks and other institutions use many different methods of calculating returns. Most are done to calculate the annual return. When you are comparing your returns to that of other investment vehicles, make sure you are using the same method as used by the institution. This will ensure a comparison of "apples to apples."

This nominal APR is the number that is calculated by the straight percentage multiplied by the number of periods in a year. Although a bank CD or a savings account is not in the same risk category as day trading, it is good to use the same mathematical method of comparing yearly returns between the two. Comparisons of APRs will allow you to more realistically judge your performance in a way that can help you determine the return of each trade.

YOUR TOTAL MONTHLY PERFORMANCE

Your total monthly performance is a truer indication as to your overall performance than how you did on any given day, since there can be good days and bad. Over time they will average out to show a more accurate performance measure. To calculate this number, take your account value at the last day of the month, and subtract the value that it was at the beginning of the month. This is your gross profit or loss for the month. From this number, subtract your expenses to arrive at a net profit or loss. This net profit/loss should be divided by the amount that was in the account at the very first day to arrive at a percentage gain for the month. The same is done for the yearly profit and loss calculations.

There are several possible scenarios:

- Your dollar amount of profit is high, you are covering your bills, and you're earning enough to draw a salary from the gains.
- The dollar amount is small, you are covering your bills associated with day trading, but you are not making enough to draw a salary.

If you are in the second of these situations, focus on the percentage returns. If they are high, but the dollar amount of the return is low, consider the fact that you are doing well and are mastering day trading; it just might be that your account balance or amount of total margin cannot produce higher dollar returns for the amount deposited. Be patient—you are doing well; it is only a matter of time before your account grows to the point of being able to throw off enough self-generated cash for you to be able to take a salary draw.

REALISTICALLY LOOKING AT YOUR PERFORMANCE

In order to realistically measure your performance in day trading you will need to look at the percentage of your monthly returns as well as the actual dollar amount of your gains. In addition to these quantitative measures there are the psychological benefits to day trading and placing winning trades in the market. You should look at the combination of these to get a feel for how you are doing in the market.

Keep in mind that it is very difficult to make consistent profits day trading at first. It might even take you a half a year or longer to learn how to consistently make a profit day trading. In this introductory period, it is really important to positively reinforce your skills. Do this by "looking at the glass half full." It is impossible to accurately set a goal as to the percentage or dollar amount you will make in any given period, whether a trading session, month, or quarter.

It depends on what trading opportunities become available, something no one can predict.

How Am I Really Doing?

Only you can answer how you are really doing. You can't really compare your returns to that of any other investment, because day trading is not a buy and hold strategy. You may find a gauge of multistrategy, multiplatform comparable returns on the benchmark Dow Jones Credit Suisse Hedge Fund Index helpful: www.hedgeindex.com.

Search out positive ways to look at your day trading experience while you are learning how to trade. If this means being happy with a $100 gain in one trading session, or a 10 percent gain in your account in one week, or even ten winning trades in a row, it is up to you to stay positive. Use the good feelings to keep yourself motivated and enthused about your new day trading career. For example, you should look at every positive experience as very good no matter how small. This is a really good habit to get into and will go a long way in keeping you motivated and learning about the markets and making fresh, well-thought-out trades.

RECORDING GAINS AND LOSSES

Accounting and Taxes

If you are planning on doing any amount of day trading, you will have to learn how to keep good records of the gains and losses in your account. You should also be keeping track of any expenses related to the production of your day trading income. These two numbers will allow you to arrive at your net income. When you use bookkeeping software, you can help your accountant simplify any tax planning she might advise.

BASIC RECORD KEEPING

You will do best when you keep a basic record of your day trading business's money inflows and outflows. A basic record can be a statement that can be kept in a notebook or on a spreadsheet such as Excel. If you have it in your plans to get an accountant for the formal preparation and assembly of your financial documents, your goal should be to make basic records of the cash ins and outs of your business.

What you are preparing is basic record keeping that is required for the preparation of an income statement. You should record expenses related to the purchase of computer equipment, office furniture, and accounting and office-related software purchases. In addition to a record of these fixed asset purchases, you should record your additions and subtractions to your day trading accounts.

You should make a list of each cash outlay and income as they occur, with positive numbers representing cash income and negative numbers representing cash outflows and expenses. The first few lines are the cash outflows related to the purchase of equipment and related costs. Each of these expenses is recorded on a separate line with a description and the amount of the expenditure listed as a negative number. You then take the receipt for the cash outflow and place it in an envelope. At the start of each week you should label and start a new envelope and place that week's expense and cash outflow receipts into that week's envelope.

The notebook should act as the main checking register of your day trading business. This means that even if you are out at the bookstore buying trading magazines and you spend money on coffee, you record the day, place, nature of expense (meals), and the cost of the item as a negative number.

If you start your day trading account with a $500, $5,000, or $50,000 deposit, you record this in the book also as a negative number, as you "spent money" on the business. In fact, it is much like you "spent" $5,000, etc., on the opening of the account, an integral part of your day trading business. Much like a business owner putting $5,000 of cash into his business account on the very first day of business, you will be doing the same: depositing the money in a "business account." In this case your business is buying and selling securities for profit. It is not exactly an expense, but it is money going out of your pocket, and this is what you are trying to keep track of: money going out, and money coming in.

RECORDING GAINS AND LOSSES

In addition to the recording of the money flows in to and out of your account, you should record the gains and losses on your actual day trading activities. If you are making more than a few trades a day, the best way to record the gains and losses in your account is to note the net gain and loss from your account on a daily basis. Write down the value of your account before each trading session. Then compare this to the amount recorded on the closing of your last trading session. Any difference between the two indicates the addition of interest that accrued from one trading session to the next. This interest should be recorded separately, as it is noted separately on a US tax return. After you take out this accumulated interest, the number you are left with is your actual trading session's starting amount.

Keep Track

Make sure you are recording additions to and subtractions from your day trading account properly. If you don't identify them on your record, you will lose track of what is profit and what are additions and subtractions of capital when you review your books during tax time.

As you trade throughout the day, you should keep track of the gains and losses that are generated with each trade. If you have a small amount of trades this can be easy to do, as you should be keeping records of your trading for review purposes. If you are doing many trades each session or you are engaging in trades that are retained from session to session such as an FX carry trade, or longer-term accumulation of a position, there is another method of recording gains and losses.

This alternate method is perfectly acceptable as far as the IRS is concerned and is often used in CPA tax preparation offices where the client is a heavy trader. In this method, your day trading account's value at the beginning of the trading session is recorded. After all of your trades are made and your positions are opened and closed, you record your day trading account's ending balance.

The account's ending balance is subtracted from the beginning balance. The end result is your net gain or loss for that trading session. This daily gain or loss is recorded in a separate book, labeled "Day Trading Gains/Losses per Session." Each session is recorded on a separate line, with the date, amount of gain or loss, and the words "day trading, various."

The combined records of your expenses, money spent on fixed assets, deposits into and out of your day trading accounts, and the record of your daily day trading gains and losses make your record keeping complete. If you keep your gains/losses record and your cash record, you are going a long way in keeping your day trading business's overall profits and losses easy to keep track of and ready for any formal document preparation.

TRADING PROFITS, EXPENSES, AND TAXES

Tracking Net Income

Even though you will be recording your gains and losses from trading, what you are actually taxed on in the United States is your net income. This net income number is your net gains minus your expenses. This section will help you determine your net income from day trading.

COMMON EXPENSES

Normal expenses can vary but usually include the costs associated with the business use of your home, any mileage you might have incurred in the process of conducting business, the portion of utilities that are attributable to the operation of your day trading business, etc. Other expenses that can be used to reduce your overall net income include any subscription services, any meals out that were related to conducting business, and any travel (separate from your mileage amount) associated with your day trading business. Almost every cost associated with the establishment, upkeep, and conducting of your day trading business can be used as an expense on your income statement. This income statement usually records the gains and losses from the beginning of the year to the end of the year at the top of the page.

Below this, list the categories of expenses related to the direct production of your day trading gains. Some of the categories are related to the business use of your home. This is usually calculated by measuring the total square footage of the home that is used exclusively for business purposes (for instance, if you have one room you use as an office). This number is divided by the total square footage of the home. The resulting percentage is the amount of your rent expenses that can be assigned as a day trading business expense.

Guide to Business Deductions

There are usually a large amount of expenses that can be attributed to your day trading business. You might be able to find some really good deductions if you consult one of the many guides to business expense deductions, including the IRS's website: www.irs.gov/businesses.

That same percentage is also taken for any shared utilities expenses, such as electricity, heat, and water. Any repairs to the building are assigned to the business at this percentage, as are condominium maintenance expenses, such as condo fees. The important thing about finding what percentage of your home is used for business is to only use the square footage of the room or rooms that serve as your office space and are used for 100 percent business. There can be no dual-usage of these parts of the home. In other words, your office must be used exclusively for business and not for personal reasons as well.

PHONE LINES AND TECHNOLOGY

Another key factor in determining if you own an actual business is if you have a phone line for the business that is separate from your personal line. Having a landline in your home fulfills the requirement of having a separate home phone, and your cell can then be used as your business line. The IRS also looks favorably on a business that has its own separate post office box, since this shows that your endeavor is an actual business.

Other expenses include the depreciation of business equipment and software. While it is best to consult the tax code, generally any business funds that are spent on equipment are expensed and deducted over a period of several years. This is called depreciation expense and the length of time and method of deduction can be determined by looking up the asset class in any number of tax guides that are available commercially.

The combination of your gains, losses, and related expenses result in what is called your net income. This net income number is the amount on which your business taxes will be based.

TAX PLANNING

In planning your taxes to take into account the profits you make day trading, you can achieve the best results by matching your gaining trades with a losing trade of equal or near equal value. While you would naturally have much more profitable trades than losing trades, matching as many trades as you can will lessen your tax bill.

For investors, this process can be done during the whole year, but when you are trading you have the advantage of matching up gains and losses with a shorter time frame, ideally with the net effect of reducing your net gains on a daily basis. Matched gains and losses can be done on a weekly and monthly basis also. This matching is usually done by the closing out of positions that are on your books that are at a loss.

Normally, if you were building up a position for a long-term trade, you would hold on to the position and continue to buy into the security as it got to lower points during the trade's holding time.

Holding the security and buying in on the dips would normally be your strategy; you might even be glad that the security fell into a loss for a short time as this would offer an opportunity to buy even more of the security at a lower price.

If you were following the tax planning method, you would weed out some of your longer-term trades that are currently losing. You would close them out at a loss if you determined that they would not turn around soon. To take tax planning further, you would make sure to do this at least once a quarter, and most of the closing out of these losing trades would be taken out in the week before the end of the quarter.

CLEANING HOUSE

"Cleaning house" serves two purposes. The first is to get the losing, nonperforming trades off of your books within a certain time limit (quarterly). The second purpose is to match your gains and losses at least once every quarter. This is important because if you are day trading full time, it is usually the custom to make quarterly estimated tax payments to the IRS. If you are matching your gains and losses, you will effectively be lowering your net income for each reportable quarter.

Your goal is always to maximize profits, yes, but keep in mind that you are getting rid of trades that are losing anyway. These are trades that are in a loss but are still on your books whether you are waiting for them to "turn around" or are engaged in some other form of wishful thinking that they will somehow turn profitable. They are losing trades—close them out, free up the money, and at least get some tax benefits from them.

On the other hand, your income statement consists of expenses as well as net gains. A goal of tax planning is to accelerate your expenses so you can claim them sooner rather than later. This means that if you are planning a new computer purchase, software upgrade, or other investment in equipment, or thinking of incurring any other expenses, it would be beneficial to incur these expenses in an earlier reporting period rather than in a later period. This is true because expenses reduce your overall net income, and this reduction of net income translates to lower taxes. To sum up, tax planning involves the reduction of your net gains by matching up your gains and losses.

This matching up has the overall effect of lowering the first part of your income statement, the net gains section, and should be done at least once a quarter. Matching up your gains and losses once a quarter allows you to pay lower quarterly estimated income taxes. It also serves to weed out the nonperforming trades on your books at least once every three months.

EXTEND YOUR KNOWLEDGE

Read, Study, and Develop

You should have a system to help you get ready for day trading session. This system can be a checklist that you go through before committing your first dollar of capital that day. This section will discuss how to keep your knowledge, learning, and trading fresh and profitable as time goes on.

STUDY FIRST, TRADE LATER

This idea applies whenever there is a certain expertise level required in a market environment. Whether you are a rare-coin dealer, a jewelry merchant, or a dealer in vintage motorcycles, if you know your product and your market well enough, you will be able to spot many buying and selling opportunities and go far with your trading business.

The same is true for day traders. You should become so versed in your field that you can check the price of a future, ETF, currency pair, or stock at any time, from anywhere, and know if it is a buying or selling opportunity. Without knowing your market, you might sometimes find yourself missing a potential money-making trade. You study the market to become an expert in it; think of it as a subject to master before taking a test. This mastery takes a lot of study and time at first, but you will quickly be able to exploit your market knowledge in both offensive and defensive ways, protecting your capital and adding to your capital through profitable trades.

MASTERING YOUR SUBJECT

After your initial study of the terms of the market and day trading, study the economy in general and the sectors specifically. When you feel as though you have a good enough understanding of how the market works, you are ready to trade. Start small at first, and try to make every trade a learning experience from spotting setups, to buy-in, to close. A day trader treats his job as a career and profession.

Keep Up with Market News

If you are going to be away from day trading for a few days or even weeks, keep track of the market news by reading www.marketwatch.com on your smartphone. If you don't keep tuned into the market, information can pass you by, as the market can change quickly.

If you do the same, you will invest in your education. This training takes time and money and means studying setups and the market as often and as regularly as possible, as well as the commitment of capital and its exposure to trades. If you were to go to a top university and get an MBA in hopes of obtaining a job as a trader in one of the big investment banks, it would take several years of full-time study and $50,000 to $100,000 in tuition expenses. Many people consider this a good investment in time and capital, as there is a potential to make a great deal of money as a trader.

Consider what others are spending in time and money in pursuit of their careers. It is good to have a reasonable expectation of how many trades it will take before you are running at full steam, making one good trade after another.

SEARCH FOR SETUPS

There are two things that are essential to a profitable day trading session: good setups and free capital to commit to the trades. If your money and margin are tied up in a grouping of positions that weren't thought out but that were entered into haphazardly, you run the risk of tying up that capital and margin in losing positions. Your goal is to preserve your capital first and to have winning trades and to make money second; you should not to trade for excitement or as an experiment. If you are going about day trading in the right way, you will have available cash and margin always waiting on the sidelines, always ready to enter into a good setup. Look for the best play of the day before you enter into a trade.

THE DAY TRADING LEARNING CURVE

Learning about the economy, the markets, and how to day trade takes time. You can expect to spend several weeks or even months to reach the point where you feel comfortable to make your first small trade. However, your real market knowledge will not set in until you have been actively day trading with actual money for several months. You may even find that after six months you are still learning the subtleties of day trading and all of the subjects that go with it, such as pyramiding, money management, and risk management.

Simplest Is Best

There is much information available out there for you to study and read to help you train for day trading. Just because someone or some company offers a complex system of trading that is difficult to learn does not mean you will have guaranteed results. The best systems are often the simplest and easiest to learn.

It is good to start your day trading off with a smaller amount of money and learn to day trade profitably before making additional deposits to your account, allowing you to trade with large account balances. This is due to the fact that it will take you time to learn to read the markets, spot setups, and technically enter and exit positions properly. It is good to give yourself time to learn the basics, as market conditions and setups usually develop slowly.

TAKE YOUR TIME

It is also good to budget your time realistically to get trained on more complicated trades. For instance, you can give yourself three months of trading equities and ETFs before moving into leveraged ETFs with 2:1 or even 3:1 ratio. After getting a good feel of how a leveraged ETF reacts to the markets, you can begin day trading some of the bear ETFs that are available. After learning how to use equities and ETFs to learn the basics of order entry, leverage, and shorting the market, you can move on to day trading Forex, which will increase your available leverage ratio (from 10:1 to 500:1) and easily give you the ability to short currency pairs. On the other hand, if after learning to read the market reports and analyze the fundamentals and technicals, you may want to move on to day trading some of the smaller-sized lots of futures, such as the e-mini S&P 500, and the e-mini commodity futures.

The overall goal is to give yourself enough time to have experiences winning and losing in the markets with a manageable amount of leverage and enough capital to feel the full emotions of day trading. Do this before moving into higher-leverage, higher-dollar accounts and riskier, faster-moving sectors. You should look at day trading as a long-term activity. With this in mind, take every precaution to ensure that you will be there to trade the next day with your account and wits intact.

INDEX